From Durham to Tehran

For Bill Hanaway
with warm regards
Mike Hillmann
Oct 91

by

Michael Craig Hillmann

Iranbooks, Inc.

Published in 1991
by

Iranbooks, Inc.
8014 Old Georgetown Road
Bethesda, MD 20814, U.S.A.
301-986-0079

Library of Congress Catalog Card Number 91-073515

ISBN-0-936347-18-X (hardcover)
ISBN-0-936347-19-8 (softcover)

Five hundred softcover copies of this first edition of
From Durham to Tehran serve as *Literature East & West* 27.
The world literature annual *LE & W* is published at the
Department of Oriental & African Languages & Literatures,
The University of Texas at Austin,
Austin, Texas 78712, U.S.A.

Acknowledgements

Part 1 of this book consists of almost daily journal entries written during October and November 1986 in Durham, England. I thank the Centre for Middle Eastern and Islamic Studies at the University of Durham for inviting me to serve as a Visiting Fellow during Michaelmas Term of that year. I especially thank Richard Lawless, J. Paul Luft, A. Reza Navabpour, and Rex Smith for their good offices. I also thank the University Research Institute at The University of Texas at Austin for awarding me a research grant that fall to write *Iranian Culture: A Persianist View* (1990).

Part 2 of this book comprises journal entries written during a three-week visit to Tehran in December 1989. I thank the Social Science Research Council for a generous grant enabling me to travel there and to Göttingen and Paris that winter to research the life of the writer Jalal Âl-e Ahmad for a still unfinished biography called *An Iranian Mullah's Son.*

Nasrollah Pourjavady helped make much appreciated arrangements for my visit to Tehran. I also thank Gertrude Nye Dorry, Parviz and Pari Ahour, Karim and Goli Emami, Ali Dehbashi, Shams Âl-e Ahmad, Mahmud Borujerdi, Simin Daneshvar, Ali Asgari, and Zohreh Ra'in for help and kindnesses which made my time in Tehran memorable and productive. I especially thank Maliheh Abbasian and her children Yashar and Sara for their loving hospitality.

From Durham to Tehran is much the better for hereby gratefully acknowledged editorial criticism and advice by my writer friends Jane Manaster and Jefferson Ranck. Anne Brokaw's word processing skills facilitated designing and editing the book.

Final thanks go, as always, to my wife Sorayya for her love and support, in this case combined with her appreciated (but not necessarily acceded to) reservations about the propriety of some personal observations in this book.

Austin, August 1991

Prologue

The aftermath of the establishment of the Islamic Republic of Iran in the spring of 1979 turned my hands-on and personal involvement with Iranian culture into ivory-tower observation from thousands of miles away. Because of the enmity between Iran and the States and because of the horrific war between Iran and Iraq, research travel to Iran on my own (that is to say, without a government invitation or sponsor) proved unfeasible to the late 1980s.

In the spring of 1982, my family and I chose London as the site for a semester's leave rather than Tehran, despite the fact that my research project called for archival and interview work in the latter city. In the summer of 1984, armed with another grant and a project really feasible only in Tehran, I had to chose Paris instead.

In the fall of 1986, another grant and semester's leave were earmarked for research on contemporary culture, for which again only Tehran was the suitable setting. My awareness of this fact during my stay at Durham University that fall gave entries in a journal I keep the flavor of reflections in a sort of academic exile. The subject of the first half of this book, those entries may strike a chord of familiarity with other Persianists far from the geographical setting of their subject of study and, for that matter, with teacher-scholars of Chinese and other literatures who deal with similar separation from the homeland of their literatures.

In late 1989, after the end of the Iran-Iraq war and after Ruhollah Khomeini's death, the opportunity to study again in Iran presented itself. The Office of Northern Gulf Affairs at the U.S. Department of State advised me officially not to travel to Iran, but unofficially expressed interest in hearing about it later. Because of a policy set by the Governor of Texas forbidding travel by state employees to Iran, I planned my trip for the winter holidays and made arrangements not to use University of Texas funding. The visa process through the Interests Section of the Islamic Republic of Iran at the Embassy of the Democratic and Popular Republic of Algeria in Washington, D.C., took eight months, probably because of

a field check in Iran to verify my addresses and
occupations during six earlier years of residence there.

For twenty days in Tehran in December 1989, I browsed
at bookstores, walked around the north side of the city,
talked with writers, and mulled over my situation as a
lover of a literature between which and me and between
native specialists of which and me barriers will always
exist. My reflections on this subject found their way into
journal entries as did my thoughts about Persian
literature studies in the States.

This book is the result of my decision to publish relevant (and substantially edited) parts of the travel diary entries from my Durham and Tehran trips, and that despite
misgivings about such a foray into the arena of creative
writing. I am not worried about displaying my obviously
limited skills as a prose stylist. But the focus on self in
writing meant for publication is unfamiliar territory for
me. I admit to egocentric aims in writing this book, among
them the wish to hang around in print (if and when all else
fails!). But *From Durham to Tehran* depicts an individual
perspective in which the testimony to individuality
should prove more central than the person(s) whose individuality receives attention. For that matter, with respect
to egocentric aspects of autobiographical impulses, as
John Steinbeck asserts in *Travels with Charley* (1962),
personal writing about trips can take on another tone, because "we don't take trips, trips take us." Moreover, I hope
that something about the texture of Iranian lives in north
Tehran today comes to the fore and eclipses even tribute to
individuality in this book. (However, this book deals with
impressions only and does not offer an analysis of
Iranian culture, which I undertake with regard to literary
Iranians in *Iranian Culture: A Persianist View*.)

This book recounts two brief parts of a continuing trip
on which I have found myself ever since boarding Pan Am
Flight 1 at New York's Kennedy Airport one evening in
September 1965. The audience I have in mind are other
such taken travellers, people who study literatures beyond
the Graeco-Roman, Judaeo-Christian pale, who find some
distant Asian literary other enriching and illuminating
and who would gladly sometimes merge with it, but know
that the trip will never allow such merging for such
foreign travellers.

A more specific audience I have had in mind while writing this book are teacher-scholars and students of Persian literature in the English-speaking world who may have answers to my questions or who may refine ideas of their own as a result of reading my impressions. My reflections on the state of Persian studies may also lead Persianist colleagues to evaluate for themselves what it is that their field is accomplishing and where it is or should be going.

* * *

Readers will hereafter notice a circumflex over the letter 'a' in some words, mostly italicised Persian terms in untranslated phrases and titles. It distinguishes between the sound /â/ as in "father" and "Tehrân" and the sound /a/ as in "hat" and "Mashhad." I also use the letter "i" in Persian words to represent the vowel sound in such words as the English "feet" and the Persian "Shirâz" and "Irân." I have not altered established spellings of Iranian names. As a further aid to pronunciation of Iranian names and other Persian words, readers should know that Persian nouns and adjectives take the stress or accent on their last syllable. Combining these notes on pronunciation, we have the correct pronunciation "ear ón" for "Irân" as opposed to the popular pronunciation of "eye ran."

I might also add a note here on the words "Irân," "Iranian," "Iranologist," "Persia," "Persian," and "Persianist." "Irân," the name of the country, derives from a word which means "of/relating to Aryans [Indo-Europeans]," while the word "Iranian" denotes a citizen or aspect of that country and its culture. An Iranologist is a person who studies the country. A Persianist studies language, linguistics, and literature in the Persian language, Iran's national language (as well as a national language in Afghanistan and the chief language in Tajikistan). The word "Persian" can refer to the language or to the culture of Persian speakers, the dominant cultural group on the Iranian plateau for nearly three thousand years.

An Iranian or Persian equivalent for the word "Persia" does not exist. It is a foreign designation for the country of Irân and derives from the Persian word *pârs* or *fârs*, which refers to the province of which Shirâz is the capital. This means that the phrase "Khalij-e Fârs," the Persian name for the "Persian Gulf," does not imply national ownership, but merely identifies that body of water as next to the province of Fârs.

Some people who persist in calling Iran "Persia" perhaps subconsciously hope for the existence of an exotic and idyllic place which has never existed. At the same time, because "Iran" has received such bad press in the West since 1978, Ehsan Yarshater, the most prominent Persianist in the English-speaking world, has argued that perhaps we should start calling the place "Persia" in the States in order to give it and its culture and people a new and fairer public relations start.

My fellow ex-Iran Peace Corps Volunteer Joseph Truskot tells the story that when he was thinking about names for an organization of ex-Iran PCVs, he opted against "Friends of Iran" (which would have paralleled the names of most country-based organizations of ex-Peace Corps Volunteers) because he was wary about the reactions of neighbors who might see mail addressed to "Friends of Iran." So we are temporarily calling our group the "Iran Peace Corps Organization" and will presumably change the name to "Friends of Iran" when our neighbors can read the phrase without seeing red.

As a final note in this "Prologue," I should address a word or two to those Iranian readers who may have heard a recent Voice of America radio program in Persian purporting to present my views of life in Iran today. The broadcast in question, based on material in Part 2 below and aired in Iran in late July 1991, misquotes me and misrepresents my impressions of Iran today. More on this in the "Epilogue."

Part 1
Durham

On the train north of York, Wednesday, October 1st.
Sunday's afternoon sun drew me to Speakers' Corner at
Hyde Park. On the grass at some distance from the several
loud throngs on the asphalt, Iranian royalists reminisced
and voiced hollow hopes. The men seemed mostly ex-
military. The women looked to have spent more of their
lives worrying about their appearance than about politics.
But 1978 had brought politics into every Iranian's life,
perhaps for always. Their meeting over, I listened to a rab-
ble-rouser from Tabriz who has stood on the same Sunday
spot for years spouting his anti-establishment fervor.
This time he refused to entertain questions from a middle-
aged Iranian man dressed nattily enough to raise the
speaker's suspicion that the man was a royalist.

During my four days in London, I browsed in the stores
around the British Museum and down Charing Cross
Road. It bothers me that #84 no longer exists. I saw my
Persian Carpets (1984) at Al-Hoda Bookstore, which
appears to have connections with the Islamic Republic.

In Room 42 at the Victoria and Albert Museum, I gave
an impromptu lecture to five Canadian tourists who
overheard me replying to a query by another tourist about
the Ardabil Shrine Carpet. They asked me to describe
what I knew and thought about it. It is a marvel, even if I
cannot quite forgive its royal origins and images it
conjures up of Shah Abbas the Great (ruled 1587-1629)
blinding his father and two sons, assassinating another
son, and blinding a grandson, all in the name of the glory
of Esfahan, which Iranians used to call "half the world."

But because the Ardabil Shrine Carpet has the most
popular of all single designs in Persian carpets, its visual
themes may speak for much of the culture: the Iranian
ideal environment as the perfect springtime garden and
the ideal order as rational and tranquil, qualities
Iranians have not found in the world about them.

While suggesting to my listeners such significance of
design, for instance, the infinity implied by field elements
disappearing under the borders, I noticed the pattern's

spontaneity for the first time. The ogival shapes extending outward from the sixteen tips of the central medallion and reaching inward from the corner quarter-medallions lack uniformity of shape. Surely one aesthetic key to Persian carpets is the spontaneity lurking behind the apparent regularity of rectilinear tribal patterns and the regularity lurking behind the apparent spontaneity of curvilinear city carpet patterns. The two approaches create an aesthetics of balance and tension called for in works of art intended to survive prolonged or repeated viewings. The Ardabil Shrine Carpet works both ways in its monumental magnificence.

Not that I was ferreting out Iran-related things during these four days except at daily sessions in the library of the School for Oriental and African Studies. I ate Italian, Tandoori, and fish-and-chips, window-shopped up and down Oxford and Regent Streets and hung out at Covent Garden where I bought a calfskin billfold and listened to music. I watched Jack Lemmon in *A Long Day's Journey into Night* at The Theatre Royal, Haymarket and afterwards dined at the new Taco Bell off Leicester Square. I spent a morning at Petticoat Lane looking at the people, after being first cheered by West Indian Gospel singers at the entrance close by the Liverpool Street Station.

On foot this morning from St. Athan's on Tavistock Place, I took the long way and walked through Mecklenburgh Square. Charles Dickens lived right off it for a while, and Virginia Woolf lived on it for a time during World War II. *Cats* has made the famous next-door Russell Square and its hotel even more famous. Then there were the first six months of 1982 which Sorayya, Elizabeth, and I spent at No. 43 William Goodenough Flats. Elizabeth attended St. George the Martyr School and played netball at Coram's Fields in the afternoons. I jogged daily around the garden track and managed to find an occasional tennis game.

That first-floor flat was the scene of special dinner parties. Sadeq Chubak came three or four times. Sandy Morton came a couple of times, once I recall with Shirin Dehghani, whom we knew from her days in Austin as an exchange student from Esfahan. Her brother Bahram was murdered during the Revolution. Their father, the Anglican bishop in Esfahan, later wrote a book about it called *The Hard Awakening* (1981). It is a sad book, both

because of his sorrow and because of his rationalization of
the event through a Christianity foreign-sounding in his
words, a Christianity that isolated him from his own
roots and people even before the Revolution.

Ebrahim Golestan came several times also, on each occasion holding forth in his engagingly imperious way on
whatever subject arose. I haven't seen him since. But our
correspondence has since filled more than one hundred-
fifty pages, mostly his long letters pleading with me to
recognize the foolishness of interest in Persian literature
of the 1960s and the inadequacy of my familiarity with
Iranian intellectual currents to study the subject.

By the time I left the Square and began the trek up
Grey's Inn Road–I should have taken the nonsentimental
route down Tavistock–my two large satchels and tennis
racket cover stuffed with papers around the rackets, and a
bursting-at-the-seams brief case were monopolizing my
thoughts.

At King's Cross Station, I located a luggage cart and my
queue. I argued briefly with a South Asian man who
almost squashed me between our carts, and then chatted
with a pensioner from York who reminisced about his
exploits in World War II. In the year 2000, will my having
spent two years as a Peace Corps Volunteer in Mashhad in
the mid-1960s qualify as an exploit? Peace Corps/Iran
closed down in '76, when the Shah decided that Iran had
progressed beyond hosting such a tangible reminder of
thirdworldness.

Durham, Thursday, October 2nd. My room at the College
of St. Hild and St. Bede–who was Hild?–boasts a dignified
high ceiling. Vertical rows of brown printed flowers over a
ribbed, beige background cover the walls. Fixings for tea
are set on a doily on a bar table next to a tall, walnut
wardrobe. To the right of the windows is a sink, above it a
white, plastic medicine cabinet with a mirror on the door.
Underneath the windows is a small, ribbed radiator. The
three windows are long, narrow, and *mehrâb*-like, extending from waist height almost to the ceiling. They com-
mand a view of the slope leading down to the River Wear
and the green University playing fields on the far side. In
the distance and to the right is a piece of the town proper.
To the left, hills lead to the countryside.

It brings to mind another room also assigned to me sight unseen, in September 1965 at the Mashhad University Club on Ahmadâbâd Street, my basement home for almost two years. That room had a view of plane trees and sunsets, and only a table, chair, bed, and a kerosene space heater in it. I can visualize its every detail and recall even the special smell of its plaster walls and stone floor that I've never smelled since.

I need to buy walking shoes, tissues, envelopes, postage stamps, and a bottle of sherry or Martini & Rossi in case guests come calling. I have relegated the tea paraphernalia to the top of the wardrobe. Iran is the only place I couldn't avoid drinking tea. I want also to get information about the region (and about St. Hild) from City Hall and later map out a schedule for the coming week without, however, lingering on the question of why a Persianist on sabbatical should even be in Northumbria to map out a schedule of work.

In this second floor guest wing, which has a sign reminding students it is off limits to them, the other residents are two Indians, who began a spirited conversation this morning before daybreak.

* * *

My only other plan for this mostly departed day is the rest of Esma'il Fasih's *Sorayyâ dar eghmâ* [Sorayya in a Coma] (1983). Although perhaps not designed as a roman à clef, in its characterizations lurk shadowy visages of Nader Naderpour, Daryush Shayegan, and others. The book is irksome in one respect: Fasih does not have his Boul Mich geography straight. It is mindful of the movie years ago called *Caravans*, which had characters entering Persepolis and exiting on to Esfahan's Royal Square. If memory serves me correctly, Galway Kinnell's novel called *Black Light* (1966) does the same thing.

Fasih's character Sorayya is taking on the personality of Iran in a coma, after the Revolution, and not likely to survive. Naderpour communicates the same sense of a culture's death in his elegiac "Sohrab and Simorgh," which he composed in honor of Sohrab Sepehri. He didn't compose it when the poet-painter died in 1980, but rather four years later, when Naderpour knew in Paris that he himself could never go back to Iran or, better, that the Iran he knew was no longer there to go back to.

The sky was an azure elegy,
the plain was ashen and sorrow-colored . . .
On the courtyard's red brick pavement
which burned in the feverish desert sun,
water seemed to have spilled from a pitcher.
Beneath that damp spot, you lay hidden in a stoneless grave
and were as nameless as desert flowers . . . Ah, Sohrab! . . .
Who supposed that after all that life-heartedness
you would sleep in the dark night of earth's forgetfulness?
You traced your lineage to two fathers:
on earth, to Sohrab; in time, to Simorgh.
The accursed name of the invincible Rostam's son
knocked you to the ground and killed you, O friend,
despite the fact that from another direction
you were the descendant of the firmament's kings,
that is to say, of the tribe of the deathless,
of the dynasty of Qâf Mountain dwellers . . .
In your eyes, morning was the smile
of a clustre of grapes dark as the vineyard.
Life was the first black figs in the acrid mouth of summer.
Waves plundered acacia petals from the river's edge.
You listened to the swallows' minstrelsy . . . and laughed . . .
Suddenly a call came from afar: Sohrab!
You leaped up and asked: Where are my shoes?
You left the house
and with the speed of wind were under the rain . . .
My troubled dream ended.
On that clear noon when I was returning from your grave,
that pure earth which embraced you,
the sky was an azure elegy,
the plain was ashen and sorrow-colored.

My call home, from the Telecard booth next to the en-
trance of the new and almost finished Milburngate Mall
by the river on North Durham Road, was cheering despite
distinct echoes, phrase by phrase, as I spoke. Sorayya and
Elizabeth are fine. Our plans for the Middle East Studies
Association meeting next month in Boston are set. I hope
we enjoy ourselves as much as we did last year in New
Orleans, as bizarre as our most carefree evening was.
Earlier that day, word reached us that Gholamhosayn
Sa'edi had died in Paris. We held a memorial service in
mid-afternoon. Then, a group of us–Sorayya, Ahmad
Ashraf, Ali Banuazizi, Jalal Matini, Habib Ladjevardi,
Farzaneh Milani, Poopak Taati, and several others–set

out for Bourbon Street and ate and drank and caroused until the early hours. Farhad Kazemi treated us to a round of beers at a jazz spot. No one mentioned Dr. Sa'edi. We had performed a New Orleans funeral.

One of these weekends I'll take a bus or coach–which is it?–to Scotland and think about my middle name. Edinburgh might be enough, although that's a city I've so far associated exclusively with the late L.P. Elwell-Sutton, one of the first European Persianists I ever met. That was at Ali Dashti's house in 1972. Mr. Dashti actually invited me to set up an exchange between Elwell-Sutton and me, which never took place because he was quiet and polite.

About what had earlier transpired between Elwell-Sutton and me, the long and short of it from his perspective was that I had done a hatchet job in my review of his translation of Dashti's *Dami bâ khayyâm* [A Moment with Khayyam]. That review in *Râhnemâ-ye ketâb* emphasized two points. First, Elwell-Sutton had translated the preface to the second edition of Dashti's book, but only the shorter, unrevised first edition of the text proper. Second, his translation wasn't error-free. Yet, some of his versions of Khayyamic quatrains read okay as verse, for example (*In Search of Omar Khayyam*, 1971, p. 188):

A drop of water fell into the sea,
A speck of dust came floating down to earth.
What signifies your passage through this world?
A tiny gnat appears–and disappears.

(I'd have used "our" instead of "your" and avoided the tautology at the beginning of the fourth line.)

However, from no-holds-barred Tehran of the early '70s, I had no idea that European and American Persianists generally avoided frank and openly critical writing about one another's scholarship. By the time I got the picture, the die was cast in terms of my approach to reviews. Unable either to keep a lid on it or to struggle to find at all costs positive features in writing on Persian literature the way Michael Beard does, I live with what disgruntled Persianists have told me and others about my reviews of their works. Six years after the fact, Ahmad Karimi-Hakkak even quoted for me a paragraph from my review of his *Anthology of Modern Persian Poetry* (1978). I hadn't remembered a line of it. Looking it over later, I saw that, among other things, I had charged him in error with mistaking the date of the publication of Forugh Farrokhzad's *Tavallodi digar* [Another Birth] (1964). Jerome Clinton wrote me ten years after my article about *The Dīvan of Manūchihrī Dāmghānī: A Critical Study* (1972) that my writing a "negative" review using a copy of the book he had given me constituted consummate gall. Gernot Windfuhr published an angry retort to my review in *Z.D.M.G.* of his work on Khayyam in *Irânshenâsi*, which had seconded my views in a short piece on recent publications. He defended his views by asserting that his earlier "brief programmatic article does ask for common sense in its own way, mainly . . . to question and put on the spot in a subtle manner (probably not caught by H.) both the distorted, Weltschmerz overridden traditional adoration of Omar, and, at the same time, the similarly boring clichées founded on the thorough misunderstanding of some of Arberry's and other scholars' substitution exercises with Persian literary symbolics. Somehow the German is too much for h." (*Irânshenâsi* 2, no. 2, Summer 1971, p. 131).

Durham, Friday evening, October 3rd. As much work on modern Persian literature has emanated in recent years from Room 26 of the Oriental Library here as from any-where else in the West.

Minoo Ramyar finished a master's thesis on Ahmad Kasravi here in the early 1970s. She then came to The University of Texas to write a dissertation on Kasravi with Ali Jazayery. That didn't work out for reasons he has never told me. But, at my suggestion, she did undertake a translation of Hushang Golshiri's *Shâzdeh ehtejâb* [Prince Ehtejab] (1969), which got published in *Major Voices in Contemporary Persian Literature* (1980).

Marziyeh Sami'i did her master's thesis here on Chubak's *Tangsir* (1963). I first met Mr. Chubak in Tehran because of that translation. He had given it to Charles Boewe at Fulbright to show it to someone for an evaluation. I read it with the original and communicated my views to Boewe, who passed along my comments to Chubak, who called to have us get together. Durham Persian Lecturer Frank Bagley later revised Marziyeh's translation, added a handful of Chubak stories, and wrote an introduction. Persian Heritage Series then published the volume.

But Chubak, who told me in London in '82 what he planned to do, protested that Ehsan Yarshater had not sought his written permission on behalf of Persian Heritage. Irritated at such objections, Ehsan removed the volume from circulation and stopped publication of Moh Ghanoonparvar's translation of Chubak's *Sang-e sabur* [The Patient Stone] (1966), which I also had a hand in, first by suggesting to Moh that he work on the novel for his dissertation project, and then by taking him to see Chubak in El Cerrito over the Christmas holidays in 1979. As for Chubak's recent change of heart and new willingness to let me arrange for the publication of both novels, I should stay out of the fray and let Moh try to salvage the situation, perhaps through Ahmad Jabbari's Mazdâ Publishers. A lingering other question is why Golestan, Chubak, and other literary men of their generation and the next resent Ehsan and his success, which he hasn't achieved at others' expense or even in competition, from far away Columbia University, with editors, writers, and scholars back in Tehran.

Another Durham graduate named Mehri Bharier wrote her master's thesis on Forugh Farrokhzad. Its reports of interviews with family members and friends and feminist reading of poems proved useful in my own research for *A Lonely Woman: Forugh Farrokhzad and Her Poetry.*

Robert Wells is a Durham County man the University let get away. When he told Mr. Bagley that his chief interest lay in Jalal Âl-e Ahmad's writings, he was advised to work with Elwell-Sutton at Edinburgh. Mr. Bagley made a mistake here in not realizing that Wells was mature enough to do the legwork himself, leaving only a critical review of his work which Mr. Bagley could have done as well as Elwell-Sutton, perhaps better because he has never been sympathetic to Âl-e Ahmad. In a letter several years ago, he berated Âl-e Ahmad for being the worst "negativist" of the whole lot of contemporary Iranian writers. He considers the resignation of the title character at the end of *Modir-e madraseh* [The School Principal] (1958) deplorable, inexcusable.

Reza Navabpour has done the most extensive work on modern Persian literature here, a wide-ranging doctoral dissertation on Persian prose writing, with good material on its *engagé* aspects. He has also published solid reviews of Mahmud Dowlatabadi's *Jā-ye khāli-ye soluch* [Soluch's Empty Place] (1979) and 3,000+ page saga called *Klidar* (1978-1983). Dowlatabadi injured his wrist in writing all of *Klidar* with Bic ball-point pens.

The best known "Durhamites" in Persian studies are Anne Katharine Swynford Lambton, who has retired to somewhere near here after her career at SOAS, and Gertrude Lowthian Bell (1868-1926), who was born in Washington Hall and authored *Persian Pictures* (1928) and *Poems from the Divan of Hafiz* (1928). Bell's life, translations, and other writing have long interested me.

Even when conjuring up personalities behind work done in Room 26 and assuming that similar heart-felt work has taken place elsewhere, I remember that English-speaking Persianists have yet to produce seminal work on the most important subjects. No critical analysis or survey of the origins of imaginative Persian literature exists. No critical history of the development of modernism in twentieth-century Persian literature from pre-modern Iranian and modernist European literary traditions exists. No one has written a critical study of the fiction of Sadeq Hedayat or any other modernist Iranian short story writer or novelist for that matter. Even Ferdowsi and Hafez are still waiting for critical appreciation based on a literary critical perspective. Except for J.T.P. de Bruijn's *Of Piety and Poetry: The Interaction of Religion and Literature in the Life and Works of Hakim Sana'i of Ghazna* (1983), no published critical study in English on a Persian literary topic comes to mind which will stand any test of time. And even de Bruijn's work is only literary critical in a tangential way.

Most of the time in Room 26 today I was getting acquainted with Basil Bunting, the Northumbrian poet who Reza Navabpour speaks so enthusiastically of. His *Briggflatts* (1966) is full of the rough "norther" outdoors and a life he thinks "Southrons" do not understand. His translations from Rudaki, Ferdowsi, Rumi, and Sa'di are clearly the work of a poet and a pleasure to read in contrast to most Orientalist versions. But for someone who had an Iranian wife, and a son named Rostam and who, Reza says, thought and talked a lot about the place, he has very little of the sights and sounds of Iran in his own verse. My favorite Bunting poem is a 1937 ode about

Samangân, the city or kingdom where Rostam sought help
after he lost his horse Rakhsh. He spent the night there
with the king's daughter Tahmineh who consequently
conceived their son Sohrab (*Collected Poems*, Oxford,
1978):

> Let them remember Samangân, the bridge and tower
> and rutted cobbles and the coppersmith's hammer,
> where we looked out from the walls to the marble mountains,
> ate and lay and were happy an hour and a night;
>
> so that the heart never rests from love of the city
> without lies or riches, whose old women
> straight as girls at the well are beautiful,
> its old men and its wineshops gay.
>
> Let them remember Samangân against usurers,
> cheats and cheapjacks, amongst boasters
> hideous children of cautious marriages,
> those who drink in contempt of joy,
>
> Let them remember Samangân, remember
> they wept to remember the hour and go.

But did Bunting remember Samangân when he named his
son Rostam? If I were to choose between the two names for
a son, I would pick Sohrab with the hope that he might
this time survive the patriarchal order of things. That
would be a country to travel to, an Iran where Sohrab's
dreams had become reality. Right would make right.
Mothers would be mentors of heroes. Reza tells me that
Bunting popularized poetry reading in pubs in northern
England. He got interested in Iran as a correspondent for
The Times.

Durham, Saturday, October 4th. On the way back from
Town Centre and dinner at a small, second-floor Chinese
restaurant whose only customers were solitary men, I
dropped a penny from Bath Bridge and thought
momentarily about Wearmouth and Bede. The penny
splashed. I smiled, a bottle of sherry in hand, just bought
and wrapped in tissue paper, and continued on my way.

In midmorning I had walked in sunny autumn warmth
to the village of Shincliffe, two miles from Durham City,
to pay my respects to Mr. Bagley. He was still in his

dressing gown. We talked for an hour. I accepted a cup of
strong coffee which I then did my best to dilute with milk.
It reminded me of the years in Iran when I accepted glasses
of tea I didn't really want. Their lingering metaphysical
aftertaste is pleasant enough, however.

Mr. Bagley and I talked about meeting at the Oriental
Library and perhaps for lunch at his college. I've been
there, to Grey College, as his dinner guest. There were
about eight of us that evening in the spring of 1982. We
were all very cheerful. The claret was especially warming.
I also remember the river of salt Mr. Bagley poured over
his food from a one-eyed salt shaker.

Today we talked about *The Encyclopaedia Iranica*, the
mid-September Orientalist congress in Hamburg,
Golestan's obstreperousness at the conference on Iran at
Durham last spring, and Chubak's curious behavior in
threatening Ehsan with lawsuits. We also talked
unenthusiastically or, better put, despairingly, about Iran.
Shi'ite clerics will orchestrate life there for years.
Ruhollah Khomeini's death will make little difference.
Iranian advocates of liberal democracy had their day in
1906 with their constitution. It has been a gradually
losing proposition ever since, despite appearances during
the Pahlavi era. Two beautiful Âbâdeh *boteh* medallion
carpets with their muted colors and almost citified
Qashqâ'i gardens distracted me from further discouraging
thoughts.

Durham, Sunday, October 5th. Two hundred "freshers" are
arriving at Bede today. Signs in the reception area direct
"monks" one way and "nuns" another. Parents are invited
to the West Common Room for tea. Bespectacled fathers,
wives seated to their left, the new university students in
the back seat, drive tentatively through the grounds to
locate a car park where they won't be threatened by a
penalty. The bursar, Mr. Wood, is standing out front greet-
ing families. "Where are you from?" "Guildford." "Well,
that's a long way."

The morning's gray mist evaporated into another
cloudless afternoon. On the hill in front of the Dining Hall
toward Main, three students wondered aloud about
trudging up it in snow. Freshers will meet for sherry in the
auditorium hall at six, among them a group from
Pennsylvania State University. At least one other

American was at lunch, laconically describing how he chose Durham, something about his parents being in Paris, his father's boss being in Cambridge, the rumor that Durham was better than London in his field of liberal arts, and finally an admission that he knew nothing about England's third oldest university.

I met a man in the basement laundromat this morning who, after a doctorate in English and nine years as editor of the *Bibliography of English Language and Literature*, is undertaking a post-graduate program in music education. He plays the piano and viol and has spent time at Terre Haute, which he informed me was the site of Indiana State University and the American office of the *Bibliography*. He speaks the same English that Dick Davis does. Maybe they teach it at Oxbridge.

Years ago, it was great fun listening to students from the provinces trying to speak Tehran Persian at Tehran University. I even made an effort once there to get Mashhad forms and pronunciation out of my own Persian. I occasionally regret not having a recognizable regional accent within America. Sounding identifiable here is a kick. Travelling has that added pleasure in feeling different and recognizable as such from those around one. That may have helped keep me enthused in Iran for so long. I felt noticeably different there.

Seated at my Edwardian windows before a greying dusk, sherry glass full of James Bell Amontillado in hand, clad in a crimson turtleneck, a blue cotton shirt worn rakishly over it, my toes testing the insides of new brown brogues from Marks and Spencer, I am carrying on this hand-to-paper-to-eye conversation with myself. Since Sorayya and Elizabeth left me in Paris on August 30th, I have re-learned how to deal with and make use of solitude, as during those early days in Mashhad. Then, of course, not knowing the language, I couldn't have talked to anyone about anything of consequence even had I wanted to. I asked myself in those autumn days of '65 what had possessed me to up and go to Mashhad. But on the face of it, that was not as bizarre as spending these six months in Paris and Durham researching a book on Iranian culture.

The question had at least one answer then, as now, which has nothing to do with Iran: the stimulating risks of deliberately chosen solitude. As Sohrab Sepehri suggests in his poems and implies in his peopleless paintings, a fine line exists between being alone and feeling alone, between solitude and loneliness. Staying near that line for long gives special feelings and teaches good lessons hard to describe to others who have not been there.

Durham, Monday, October 6th. I spent the morning at the Oriental Library rereading Gustave von Grunebaum's pieces on Arabic literary aesthetics. Edward Said is right about him in *Orientalism* (1978). He was a scholar galvanized by disdain for the subject and people he studied and wrote about. But Said is off target in implying that Persianists today have a similar attitude. True, I have limited sympathy for Islam as a social institution and as the essential force in the lives of Iran's illiterate majority. I am also indifferent to as many Iranians as I like. The point is that Persianists worth their salt recognize that Hafez is as good as poets get, that Âl-e Ahmad can write as bold an essay in as distinctive a style as any writer anywhere can, and that Sadeq Hedayat's *Buf-e kur* [The Blind Owl] (1937, 1941) succeeds in creating atmosphere as well any narrative could. In short, Persian literature is worth studying because it is first-rate. It is first-rate because Iranian culture and writers have what it takes.

From the Oriental Library, I walked back towards South Road to the Centre to pick up my mail. The building is an eighteenth-century inn hovering over the old Main North Road. They've assigned me a cozy, garret-like office on the third floor, under the eaves. From its window I can look out and imagine a carriage from York bringing news of the Sepoy Mutiny. That the very first telegraph line in Iran connected Tehran to London hints at how skewed views of Iran can get. Even Iranians now think it natural to call their region *khâvar-e miyâneh* [the Middle East].

I walked down South Road, past University Library, to Church Road and from there to City Centre and Marks and Spencer on Silver Street, just below Market Place. With a store-bought lunch from M&S, I returned to my room at Hild-Bede, where I read Shams Âl-e Ahmad's *Gâhvâreh* [The Cradle] (1975). The old Tehran family environment he depicts mirrors settings in Jalal's autobiographical stories. It has always appealed to me as an authentic Iranian environment: Reza Shah was an enemy, but at least a worthy adversary, unlike his short-sighted, arrogant and ineloquent son. Oriana Fallaci's *Interview with History* (1976) offers incontrovertible evidence for such an indictment of the man who led Iranians to the brink of revolution. Fathers were dictatorial and religion-bound between the world wars, yet somehow principled. Iran was in a desperate state, not despairing yet of its cultural identity. Khomeini's arch-enemy was never Mohammad Reza Pahlavi, but rather the latter's father Reza Pahlavi.

Durham, Tuesday, October 7th. Last night I had trouble getting to sleep. Strange, fleeting sensations in the chest kept me wide awake. I remember a dozen such evenings at William Goodenough House in '82, when I would spend an hour sneaking beneath or behind the sensations to get to sleep. At the time, I assumed my anxiousness at getting material on Farrokhzad was triggering the feelings. The project was stressful all the way. Interviewees were suspicious. Some wondered why I had chosen Farrokhzad (and not themselves?) as the subject of a book. Mr. Golestan didn't once mention her by name that spring during a dozen conversations, all the while knowing that I had sought him out precisely because of his relationship with her. In addition, some mornings, while racing page-by-page through issues of *Ferdowsi* magazine at the School of Oriental and African Studies Library, I would get almost out of breath and look up to see if the sound of my heart beating was distracting library patrons nearby.

In retrospect, the sensations were worth it. *A Lonely Woman: Forugh Farrokhzad and Her Poetry* expresses personal convictions, and communicates my sense of Farrokhzad's views on people, relationships, and issues, and my concurrence, which Messrs. Golestan, Alavi, Baraheni, Jamalzadeh, Mahmud Enayat, and others may not like. They shouldn't, because it is their patriarchal subculture disguised in modernist garb which Farrokhzad indicts in the book through my words. Some Iranian Persianists in the States may likewise feel uncomfortable with the book's implied point. There is nothing I could do about it. Halfway into the project, Farrokhzad convinced me of the insightfulness of her views on Iranian life and art and of the integrity of her bold individuality.

As for last night, either the coffee in the morning or anxiety about not being on the same wave lengths as Iranian scholar friends may have prompted sleeplessness.

Yesterday, I had a letter from Heshmat Moayyad, who politely and indirectly complained that my review of his translation of Jamalzadeh's *Yeki bud yeki nabud* [Once upon a Time] (1985) was unfair. I read the letter seated on the stone ledge by the entrance to the Centre and did not relax again until I had answered it back at Hild-Bede. Although I had no criticism of the translation itself, I couldn't resist wondering aloud in the review about the relevance of the book itself and its translation sixty years after its Berlin publication. Because Heshmat was my professor and is a friend, perhaps I should not have wondered aloud about his book.

Behind that wondering lies an issue not raised in the review: the tendency of Iranian Persianist scholars to shy away from rigorous biographical inquiry into their favorite poets and other writers. When *A Lonely Woman* appears next spring, it will be the first biography I know of on a major Iranian literary figure. Heshmat's chapter in *Once upon a Time* called "Jamalzada's Life and Works" carefully sidesteps biographical issues. Donné Raffat's *The Prison Papers of Bozorg Alavi: A Literary Odyssey* (1985) is equally circumspect in its treatment of a more controversial writer. Nader Naderpour's silence about my *False Dawn: Persian Poems* (1986) implies his displeasure at my biographical introduction. Why Iranian literary artists don't write autobiographies and why they don't appreciate biographies are significant pieces in the Iranian cultural mosaic.

Durham, Wednesday, October 8th. Before dawn, the Indians in Guest Room #2 were jabbering away, which I guess is what awakened me. That was okay, although after an excursion yesterday to Newcastle and hours of walking there, I could have slept until noon. I'm now shaved, dressed, and ready for breakfast and work, and it's only seven-thirty. Outside whooshes a blustery wind through layers of marbled grey in the sky. After nine American Indian summer days, today looks to be a lesson in Durham's fabled bad weather. In anticipation of a deluge, I have applied almost daily coats of waterproofing spray to my new shoes.

These unhurried days, when time nevertheless hurries along, have me trying to slow things down through the self-conscious savoring of routine activities, shoe spraying included, activities often otherwise hastily accomplished to get to supposedly more important things. But things aren't temporally more or less important when they use up the same amount of time and life. I think about what's happening when I floss and brush my teeth, wash and dry my clothes, walk from my room to downtown–that's easy here, the lines, shapes, angles, and colors are so striking–eat simple meals, take baths, and engage in momentary exchanges at shops, the post office, and the bank. French worship of food, Spanish siestas, American window-shopping, English appreciation of a sunny day, and Italian talking suggest that plenty of people have discovered bits of this obvious secret. I used to think Iranians were good at it too. Naderpour has a poem from the early 1970s called "Breakfast," which goes:

> All my morning life is this:
> after opening eyes,
> washing hands and face in the mirror's spring water.
> After seeking light's blessing,
> beating dawn in the yolk of a raw egg,
> drinking wet breeze with fresh milk.
> After freeing the body,
> tying imagination to the soaring of birds,
> breaking away from everything,
> going, joining myself.

In his daily life, Naderpour has long instinctively confronted and violated time. He rarely gets ready on time, can spend minutes looking at unopened mail, loses (or finds) himself in front of the mirror, and washes his hands and cigarette lighter just for the hell of it.

* * *

During today's jog along the river's edge, the grey almost blustery weather gave an edge to the sunlight, as did the freshly mowed playing fields directly across the river from Hild-Bede. On the walk back, I watched single sculls and eights practicing on the Wear. The eights are herky-jerky now, the beginning of the training season. From my room, I can see them for moments between the trees. In six years in Iran, the size of eleven or twelve Englands, I saw running river water only three times, on trips to Esfahan. Ahvâz, site of Iran's one navigable river, never appealed to me enough to get me there, although the place seems alive in poems by Forugh Farrokhzad and Feraydun Tavallali, especially the latter's "Kârun."

As calm as a carefree swan
the small boat plied the Karun.
The sun was sinking into the horizon
at the palm grove along the shore.

Playful in the water's rippling,
the twilight had a special splendid secret.
The breeze seemed to creep along
a plain of poppies intoxicated.

Paddling through crests of waves,
a young man moved the boat along.
His heart-and-soul was in the boat.
His sorrow-sick voice joined the wind:

"Your tresses are my rebec's strings.
What can you want from my ruinous state?
Why do you who feel no love for me
come late every night to my dreams?"

In the boat, a woman's tresses
gently curled in the evening breeze.
She leaned from the boat
and dragged her finger in the water's wrinkles.

Sounds gently spread out in every direction
like the fragrance of a rose in the breeze.
Filled with a warm sorrow
the youth sought a caressing hand in song:

"You who are not my nectar, why do you sting me?
You who are not my friend, why are you next to me?
You who are not salve for my heart's wound,
why are you salt for my wounded heart?"

There was silence, and in the moonlight
the woman's face was blue like the color of night.
Happy, content at the young man's suffering,
her head was with him, her heart elsewhere.

From the other direction of the Karun came
another small boat, light on shimmering waves.
A light flickered in the reedbed.
A plaintive voice sang from afar.

A passing breeze brought this message:
"How joyous is affection from two directions."
The young man moaned under his breath in regret:
"One-sided love is tribulation."

Not that I buy Tavallali's poem hook, line, and sinker:
why is the woman in the boat? But he creates a palpable
Karun.

Durham, Thursday, October 9th. At the Oriental Library
today I mostly studied Ferdowsi, at one point reading pas-
sages from the story of Rostam and Sohrab half-aloud,
there being no one else in Room 26. For the first time, the
Shāhnāmeh seemed closer to *Beowulf* in spirit and
technique than to *Aeneid.* Because Ferdowsi was a self-
conscious city poet versifying and embellishing an exist-
ing prose version of Iranian epic stories, his proximity in
tone and technique to Western primary epics as opposed to
secondary epics deserves comparatist attention. I had
pulled a *Shāhnāmeh* off the shelf, the 1976 reprint of the
Jules Mole edition, after coming across an article in a
festschrift called *Logos Islamikos: Studia Islamica in
honorem Georgii Michaelis Wickens.*
    The article which caught my eye was called "The
Tragedy of Sohrab" and mistakenly asserts: that
Tahmineh, fearing that Rostam might take their son
Sohrab away from her, lied to him in a letter about
Sohrab's size; that Gordafarid sent the famous letter
which got King Kavus to summon Rostam back to the
court; that Sohrab was Rostam's only son; that Sohrab
deserves blames for his own death; and that Rostam, who
continues on his martial way once the Sohrab episode is
over, is a tragic hero. Such misreadings and
misstatements of facts are less troubling than the *a priori*
view about Rostam and his son, a gratuitous assumption
that right lies with the father. Why do some Persianist
scholars want to view Rostam as a righteous victor over
his son? To justify establishment activities? To
rationalize that Iranians are governable only with a
king?
    On the walk down Elvet Hill, I pondered the prospect of
Persian studies influencing truer and richer views of
Iranian culture. Its openmindedness and willingness to

treat past and present as on an equal footing do constitute steps forward. Ehsan Yarshater's forthcoming *Highlights of Persian Literature* will raise traditionalist eyebrows. It devotes more space to Farrokhzad than to any single classical poet, and as much space to the twentieth century as to the whole classical period. Contemporary prose fiction receives as much attention as the medieval *ghazal.*

But, we aren't producing consistently sound scholarship. For example, George Morrison's *History of Persian Literature from the Beginning of the Islamic Period to the Present Day* (1981) neither does what its title promises nor treats medieval and modern literature with anything approaching scholarly accuracy. We do little serious textual criticism. Iraj Bashiri's edition of Hedayat's *Tup-e morvari* [The Pearl Cannon] (1986) will evoke little but derision on the part of Tehran-trained Persianists. We aren't even introducing the classics accurately or stylishly. Reuben Levy's *The Epic of the Kings* (1967) is merely the lengthiest example of unsuccessful translations from medieval Persian verse.

Not that I have a right to point an accusing finger at others. I still know much less about Persian literature than I did about English as a graduate student at Creighton in 1963. I felt very comfortable then in the company of Wordsworth, Tennyson, Milton, Shakespeare, Hopkins, Eliot, Hemingway, Frost, and others, and had read and thought about almost everything they had written.

As for what keeps me in Persian literature, three reasons have little to do with the fact that the best of Persian literature may be literature at its best. First, there is Sorayya. Second, I have always wanted to experience "the other" aesthetically and culturally, to make better sense of my own situation and future; and fate got me to Iran at an impressionable age. Third, when I first saw Twelver Shi'ite Islam in action in Mashhad and realized that it was an Arabic-Persian translation of the Latin-English Roman Catholicism of my childhood and youth, I lost the ability to imagine and talk to God. I probably can't leave Persian literary culture until I find Him again.

A critic for whom the text is the central fact and is *sui generis*–Elder Olson's Theory of the Lyric course at Chicago sold me on a formalist approach–, I nevertheless leave the text whenever necessary and find non-literary or extrinsic values in literary texts, for example, their function as self-views into culture. I do not treat texts objectively, but rather announce my American, male ethnocentrism and suggest to readers and students that my explicitly ethnocentric perspective can lead them to see things in a new light and decide for themselve the nature and value of those things. My practical approach in reading and writing is to discern critical issues and questions and to frame tentative answers to them. Robert Beum got me started on critical papers in a Milton course at Creighton. What accounts for unity in Hafezian *ghazals*? What does *The Blind Owl* mean? What is female about Farrokhzad's lyric verse? Why do Western readers not find Ferdowsi's *Shâhnâmeh* literarily appealing or effective? How can a contemporary American enjoy medieval Persian court panegyric verse? At the same time, I gravitate toward major authors and major issues, implying to readers and students that they might consider asking their own critical questions, focus their gaze on critical issues while broadening their horizons, and choose significant issues to address.

Although not a first-rate scholar and although lacking the instinctive feel and wealth of background which Iranian-born literary critics can have, I believe wholeheartedly in scholarship as a process. Moreover, because I came to know Iran by living there and only chose a career in Persian Studies after experiencing the literary scene in Tehran and life there and in Mashhad and elsewhere, my unpatronizing, unromantic commitment to contemporary Iranian writers and their works and to classical Persian poetry may give my writing and teaching a distinctive perspective. Long hours of socializing with Iranian writers, together with the special attention I give to literary criticism produced in Iran, may have given me a distinctive appreciation of imaginative Persian literature as primarily both a living window into culture and an expression of live, relevant art.

At mid-career, specific projects in mind for the future give me energy and a sense of anticipation. There'll be a new book on Hafez, an anthology of translations of Persian literary classics, and a book on cultural messages in Iranian visual arts. In addition, I plan to research, think about, and write in principally three areas: first, on theories of Persian aesthetics, particular the nature of poetic statement, and the cultural ramifications of

possibly culture-specific aspects of that aesthetics;
second, on my conception, as treated suggestively in
Iranian Culture: A Persianist View, of the arguably
dipolar nature of Iranian literary cultural attitudes; and,
third, on cultural biographies, such as my work on
Baraheni, Âl-e Ahmad, Naderpour, Farrokhzad, and
Nima Yushij.

And I love teaching, a job which has never felt like
work to me. The bell at the end of class almost always
surprises me in the middle of convincing others of the
richness of experiencing that Iranian "other," through
that other's texts, from the Achaemenid ruins of
Persepolis to Sa'edi's *Chub-be dasthâ-ye varazil*
[Clubwielders of Varazil], from the Boston Hunting Carpet
to Parviz Kalantari's paintings of village scenes, and even
some medieval panegyric verse, for me the least inviting
sort of Persian literary text. Farrokhi's "Caravan of
Robes" *qasideh* is a classic illustration:

> I left Sistan, on a caravan laden with clothes,
> carrying a heart-spun, soul-woven robe,
> a silken robe, its fabric speech,
> a patterned robe, its design language,
> its every warp drawn laboriously from my mind,
> its every weft separated with great effort from my soul,
> a trace in it of every rhetorical device you could wish,
> an example in it of every verbal novelty you could seek.
> Not a robe which water can damage or fire ruin.
> Neither the dirt of the earth can harm its color,
> nor the passage of time obliterate its design.
> I organized and penned it quickly in my heart,
> and cajoled thought to be its guardian.
> Intellect would bring me the good news hour by hour:
> "This robe will bring you fame and fortune."
> This robe is not woven with robe material–
> Do not think of it in comparison with other robes.
> This robe language shaped, wisdom formed, intellect wove;
> I put both hand and heart into it.

To this point I can entertain Farrokhi's mood and points
without too great a stretch. At the core of his Persian aesthetic lies decorative complexity, interwoven embellish-
ment, dazzling ornament. One can't relax in Iranian literary culture until developing a taste for it. That done, however, the Persian aesthetic has another surprise, adjust-

ment to which remains an ongoing process for me. It is the rhetoric of praise, lavish, hyperbolic encomiasm for the powers that be. Farrokhi continues his *qasideh* with these words:

> Its design executed, at its head I wrote:
> In praise of Abolmozaffar, Shah of Chaghaniyan,
> Prince Ahmad Mohammad Shah, refuge of the army,
> that country-conquering, world-seizing monarch . . .
> The sun always revolves around his throne,
> this eye of the sky always looks toward his abode.
> Fearing for itself, Mercury becomes dark in the firmament,
> if on a day of battle the king stretches a hand toward a quiver.
> Woe is he who turns his head back from obeisance,
> his head becomes a spear tip's crown on the battlefield . . .
> One day the lustre of your blade shone on a fire
> which in fear of that blade hid in stone.
> So now when you strike a rock with iron,
> sparks fly and leap into the world . . .
> For as long as air is about us and earth beneath our feet,
> it will be air's nature to be light and the earth's to be heavy.
> May your nature, another air, be as light as the air.
> May your dignity, another earth, be as weighty as the earth.

Even if one supposes that Farrokhi here has in mind depiction of a kingly ideal and encouragement of a less than ideal king to live up to an unattainable ideal, it is a long journey from a late twentieth-century October evening at Hild-Bede College to a mid-eleventh-century royal court scene in distant Khorasan. More important trips may also be there for taking. Still, the Orient Local into and through literary Shirâz, Tus, Samarqand, Bokhârâ, and Ghazneh has its pleasurable sights and memorable stops.

Scotland, Friday, October 10th. The last few kilometres in England were breathtaking: first, stands of evergreens with browned-out ferns underneath, then rolling hills for miles around with dried clumps of ferns. Sheep were everywhere, surrounded by simple stone walls. A sign said: "Scotland Lookout 400 Yards." Above the rise to the north, as if the Tourist Board could have planned it, came another change, different greens and browns as far as the eye could see (farther than Fremont, Nebraska, seen from Mt. Michael Abbey at Elkhorn) and a glorious sun. The le-

gend in a British Tourist Authority *Map for Motorists* in-
forms readers: "Areas of Outstanding Natural Beauty are
marked for England and Wales only, as most of Scotland,
by virtue of its landscape, can be classified as such."

We are now standing at the station at Jedburgh. I've
been craning my neck this way and that, peering into
people's gardens, sitting room windows, the cemetery, half
expecting to see something about my Craig ancestors. I
can't see anything that would have made me leave with
other Scottish Presbyterians, first for Northern Ireland
and then for Londonderry, New Hampshire, in time for
one of those ancestors to have signed the 1770 petition for
the incorporation of Pondtown Plantation in the
Massachusetts Bay Colony, one portion of which
thereafter became Readfield. But he did. My great great-
grandfather Thomas J. Craig was born in Readfield in
1803 and married Nancy White in 1826. The had four
children: Mary Ann, Charles Augustus, Elizabeth Nancy,
and my great-grandfather Horace Thomas. He was born in
Searsmont in 1832 and married Elizabeth Keating. They
had three children, two girls who died young and
Grandfather David Craig, who was born in 1870. In youth,
his widowed mother took him to Montana for his health.
He became a cowboy, more likely and literally a sheep
herder. Jim keeps Grandfather Craig's six-shooter by his
bed in Baltimore. When Great-grandmother Craig had a
stroke out west, David brought her back to Searsmont to
what we have always called the Red House, right across
from Fred Miller's Store (Ben Ames Williams uses other
names for Searsmont's people and places in *Fraternity
Village*). I never met Grandfather Craig, who died in 1937.

Edinburgh, Saturday, October 11th. After a meandering
walk from the University Main Library where I spent two
hours skim reading Robert Wells's 1982 thesis on Âl-e
Ahmad, I ended up at a cheery basement Italian restaurant
on Hanover Street. I had been on the lookout for a Scottish
restaurant, but was getting cold walking. The Castle,
which I saw at dusk and then again illuminated at night,
was imposing. I tried calling Sorayya from Waverly Train
Station, but got no answer.

What I saw from before Jedburgh through Melrose,
where Cuthbert was prior, and Golashiels almost into
Dalkeith and the city was as beautiful as landscapes can

be. The undulations and rounded tops of hills, the visible
miles into the distance, the demarcations of color made by
field divisions, crops, ferns, the off-white sheep ready for
shearing against the lawn green beneath and behind them,
the clean, sharp angles of homes with well tended lawns
and neat flower beds, the glassy clear brooks, the trees
turning almost to brown, and the ribbon of narrow road
flowing with the lay of the land–it was moving even,
especially after a New Waver's radio in the back of the bus
could no longer get a London rock station.

Finding Wells's thesis has been icing on a weekend
cake. It cites facts I need as well as salient data from interviews with Shams Âl-e Ahmad, Simin Daneshvar, and
Parviz Daryush. I should write Robert to see if he has pur-
sued his interest in Âl-e Ahmad. Someone told me he now
works for Oxfam in Oxford. He says Farrokhzad was one
of the younger writers who used to go to Âl-e Ahmad's
house. I doubt this. Also, he doesn't consider cultural in-
consistencies in his subject, although he has made a good
analysis of Âl-e Ahmad's participation in the Tudeh
Party, and of *Gharbzadeqi* [Weststruckness] (1962, 1964)
and *Dar khedmat va khiyânat-e rowshanfekrân* [On the
Services and Treasonable Activities of Intellectuals]
(1978).

This morning there's not a cloud in either sky, mine or
Edinburgh's. My plans call for a walk to Pringle's tweed
and tartan factory outlet on Bangor Street on the other
side of the city, with stops at John Knox's house and St.
Mary's Cathedral on the way. Then back to Charlotte
Square, a stroll down the Royal Mile, a look-see at what
Waverly Market is all about, and back to my room to rest
and write before dinner. After a shower and shave, I'll either try a restaurant in this southside community or
stroll back to the University neighborhood.

The University has bold modern buildings alongside
castle-like structures. James Thin is a wonderful
bookstore. George Square was impressive, as were the
country and surrounding buildings that front South
Bridge Road. The University library seemed first-rate.
American accents are everywhere on campus. The
librarians were disarmingly helpful–one went herself to
get Wells's thesis when I told her, No, I couldn't "come back
on Monday" in this decade.

My room at the Sylvern Guest House at 22 West
Mayfield barely holds a bed, dresser, and wardrobe, and a
guest. But it's bright and tidy, and awash with comforters
and blankets, on the bed, in dresser drawers, on the closet
shelf. The single second-floor bathroom serves six rooms.

* * *

I called Sorayya today from cavernous Waverly
Station, a great hubbub about me in the Travel Centre.
Two people were waiting to use the card telephone after
me. It was nine in the morning in Austin. Sorayya
answered the third time I dialed, using a Telecard with
forty-nine units left on it. The din of the crowd and
intermittent announcements on the public speaking
system made it hard to hear her. She said every thing was
okay at home. Then she said, "I wrote to you two days ago."
Strange of her to mention it. She continued, "I wrote to you
about Carter, Carter Bryant." "What about Carter?" "He has
died." "What? How?" I couldn't hear what Sorayya next
said, except that she repeated that everything was in the
letter. We cut short our conversation when the blinking
indicator reached unit 1. I hung up and, with Carter on my
mind, walked toward the Silvern down North Bridge,
which becomes South Bridge, which becomes Nicholson.

He couldn't have been much over forty, and always on
the brink of recognition for one of his many talents. He
could (should?) have made it as a stage actor. Ditto for a
foreign service career, wherever cultural sensitivity and
consuming interest in people were priorities. Eventually,
he might have been known as an exceptionally creative
translator of modern Persian prose.

The Persianist establishment never warmed to Carter
or appreciated his translation of Baraheni's *Ruzgâr-e
duzakhi-ye âqâ-ye ayâz* [The Infernal Days of Mr. Ayaz]
(1972). Of course, the establishment then was officially
pro-Pahlavi, while the novel recounts the royal
sodomization of a nation. Carter published equally sensitive translations of stories by Âl-e Ahmad, Hedayat, and
Chubak in various anthologies. He was best as a counsel-
lor to younger people. Indefatigable and sympathetic, he
knew especially well problems which Iranian students
face in the States.

I first heard of him in October 1966. He had trained in
the Iran Peace Corps Program at Texas that summer,

where I had trained the summer before. He was a target for the UT Tower sniper Charles Whitman shortly after lunch one day on the South Mall. He later told me he hid under a bush during the shooting. Carter was never in exactly right places at exactly right times.

Peace Corps/Tehran assigned him to the Iranian high school system in Torbat-e Jâm in September 1966, as I began a second year of teaching English at Mashhad University. John Newton, my suite-mate at the University Club the year before, had just returned to Iran as the field officer for eastern Iran, which included Torbat-e Jam and Mashhad. The two places don't belong in the same sentence. Mashhad, as Iranian and as far from Tehran as it was, at least had a university, a group of secular-minded intellectuals, a night life at the Bâkhtar Hotel, Foruzan Farrokh's crowd of hip university students who knew the Beatles and partying, and the restaurant at Kuhsangi. Doug Fossek, John's replacement at the University, and I spent occasional Thursday evenings at Kuhsangi eating a leisurely dinner and listening to a live band. You could get a vodka and Seven-up with a twist of lemon there. And I had my own group of friends who met at the Bakhtar, and basketball and tennis, and even occasional dates.

Word reached Mashhad that the new American in Torbat was blending in. The students liked him. The English teachers liked him. The local teachers, engineers and such were ecstatic at finding such a *sympa* listener and drinking buddy and, as Carter later told me, a sometimes fellow traveller at opium sessions.

By the summer of 1970, Carter had become Director of the Iran-America Society in Mashhad. He did great things with what formerly wasn't a lot more than a public relations arm of the United States Information Service. He made a movie during this period called *Châdor*, a silent motion picture of a day in the life of a *châdor* veil being taken to the dry cleaner's. Most of it is still on videotape, if not on the original 8 mm film. According to Carter, at one point what he assumed were SAVAK agents poured acid on the original film stored in a desk drawer at home. Carter shot one scene from atop a moving taxi cab. He fell off and had multiple stitches in his chin thereafter to show for his dedication to the cinema.

In March '71, Peace Corps/Iran staged a grand Persian language conference in Mashhad. Mike Jerald made arrangements with Carter to use IAS as conference headquarters. Over fifty volunteers from all over Iran turned up for the two-week affair, among them Bruce Linden from Ahar and Joel Hettger from Tehran. The Turkophilic Peachys, not happy about having to travel through "Persian" country, took various buses from Khoy. A crowd came by chartered bus from Peace Corps headquarters in Tehran. The chief carrots accompanying the intensive language learning sticks were a camel ride which my brother-in-law Javad and a Mashhad University Medical School classmate of his arranged outside Old Nishapur and a conference-ending trip to Herat. When I visited Herat for a weekend in late '72, merchants were still talking about the dozens of Persian-speaking Americans who descended cheerily upon the Herat bazaar that April with money to burn.

Carter persuaded an Iranian friend who had managed an Italian restaurant in Massachusetts to cater the whole two weeks. So we feasted on Italian-American cuisine. A local carpet merchant named Ahmad Farshchian provided Persian carpets for all conference rooms. We laid them down wall-to-wall in the Society's auditorium, which became a dormitory for single men. Women and couples and families stayed in Society offices and in classroooms equipped with space heaters and beds. Ahmad proceeded to fall in love with Parvaneh Âmon, one of our language teachers, to no avail. And he was nervous as hell when he gave his Persian lecture on carpets to the conference participants.

The first busload of PCVs arrived six hours early from Tehran to the cheers of the passengers who had encouraged the driver to fight off sleep and pass by scheduled rest stops. I rushed to IAS from my in-laws' house where I was staying. There were only momentary snags. Carter had put the whole thing together like a theatrical production. Many of those fifty PCVs–and Gene Garthwaite and his family, and Bill Beeman–surely remember that conference as a special and rewarding time.

As IAS Director during a time when the American government no longer assigned a consul to Mashhad, Carter became the official American there. During those days of world travellers, hippies, and drug smuggling, Carter was the lifeline for Americans caught with drugs and sentenced to languish in the Mashhad prison. He also took in strays and made himself available to every foreigner in Khorâsân needing help. I next saw him in 1974 in Austin, where he had returned to do a Persian Ph.D. at Texas.

In the interim one other experience had Carter's signature on it. As an entertainment at the Mashhad workshop, he had brought the male Sufi dancers from Torbat-e Jam to a party at Karim Sheshliki Restaurant at the out-of-town garden area called Coca Cola. They danced for their dinner. Two years later in Tehran, Sorayya and I saw the same dancers, now choreographed with women as well, performing at Rudaki Hall. Carter had introduced Iran to an expressive manifestation of its own culture. He later had mixed feelings about what had happened to the Torbat dancers and their traditions once Tehranized.

In the spring of '74, Texas advertised for an assistant professor of Persian. Sorayya, three-year-old Elizabeth and I had returned from Tehran the previous September, mostly at Sorayya's insistence, for me to finish my dissertation at Chicago. Bruce Craig gave me a job that year as Persian cataloger in the Near East Department at The University of Chicago Library. Texas invited me for an interview, with Carter as my unofficial host during my three days in Austin. He was then teaching at the Intensive English program and taking graduate courses in Persian with Ali Jazayery. Ray Cowart was also there at that time, Carter was full of energy and enthusiasm.

Texas offered me the job only after, as Ali Jazayery later told me, Wheeler Thackston turned it down for a position at Harvard, where he remains. His translations of Naser Khosrow's *Book of Travels* (1986) and Ansari's *Intimate Conversations* (1978) are stylish. I've never had occasion to use his *An Introduction to Persian* (1978). Paul Luft uses it here at Durham. Another Persianist opening I had my eye on that year was at Columbia. Colin MacKinnon, from our Texas 1965 Peace Corps training group, got that job, but stayed in teaching for only a year or two. He has written a novel on Iran called *Finding Hoseyn* (1986). Columbia has yet to fill that junior Persian position.

Sorayya, Eliza, and I drove to Austin by way of Baltimore in late August 1974, most of our worldly possessions in a brand-new, forest green, two-door Chevrolet Vega sedan. We felt good to be starting something without much baggage. I was raring to do big (and as yet unaccomplished) things in Persian studies.

Back at the Silvern now, I plan to pile on the comforters and have them live up to their name.

Durham, Sunday, October 12th. Up at dawn, I had to knock on the landlady's door at the Silvern for twenty minutes to pay my bill, all £8 of it. Then came the two-mile walk to St. Andrew Square. On the way, I stopped at a grocery shop for a banana and a *Sunday Times*. Do South Asians own all of the small grocery shops in the United Kingdom? I boarded the eight-thirty coach to Durham. The driver persuaded me to take it, rather than the speedier nine o'clock express, by referring scornfully to the latter's route down A1 or A9, whilst his coach would enjoy the tourist route, the same Route 68 I had come north on. Another cloudless morning watched over the again magnificent Cheviot Hills. Carter and the Craigs buzzed in the back of my mind. The sun, the scenery, a leisurely read of *The Times*, snacks of salmon *paté*, oat cakes, and a tin of carbonated apple juice, and a sense of physical well-being from many miles trekked in Edinburgh all conspired to bring on sleepy contentment.

Back in Durham by early afternoon, I felt full of happy and sad secrets on the walk through town and across the river to Hild-Bede. No calls and no messages, I unpacked, thought about sitting down to write, and then decided to jog. After a run along both sides of the Wear, I took a hot bath. Thinking the better of going to high tea at the Dining Hall, I set out for La Stalla Ristorante. A mushroom pizza, tossed salad, and a half-litre carafe of the house red wine later, I am in the mood to write.

Just before dusk a sudden chill in the air joined forces with a clear and cloudless sky, and an impressionistic mist began to shroud the town, giving the Cathedral and Castle an air of mystery and making the Wear seem eirily tranquil. A four-person scull from one of the colleges was still slicing through the water, the rowers scooping pieces of it in unison to propel their narrow boat forward. My left hand, holding an aerogramme, was cold by the time I got to Silver Street and the Post Office.

I had "Craig" looked up in Edinburgh–Crag, Craggie, and Craig are variants of a Scottish equivalent to "Smith" in popularity–and got a geneological printout from Pringle's

computer. I sent Jim a Craig tartan plaid necktie.
Elizabeth would have liked the New Wave clothing shops
on Cockburn Street, Pepe shirts everywhere. Waverly
Market, next to the Station, is modern and mall-like.
Sorayya would have liked it and most of Princes Street.
For me, Charlotte Square, the Royal Mile, the University
campus, the firth in two directions, the barren Salisbury
Crags nudging the city's flanks, the grey stone homes on
the south side, many of them now guest houses, and the
friendliness all over town will make for memories. I had
fun talking with the Iranian owner of an army surplus
store where I bought an orange Wynnster backpack. He
thought it magic that Persian sentences could come out of
the mouth of a blue-eyed, Mick-faced American. The one
cloud in the sky was the news of Carter's death.

During the '74-'75 school year, we had a furnished
apartment at a nondescript complex called Brownstone
where Elizabeth learned how to swim in the courtyard
pool. Elizabeth's English was fluent by then, after nearly a
year in Chicago. Sorayya went back to college, eight years
after her one year at Mashhad University.

That year, Carter included us in his crowd's activities:
swimming and tenting at Lake Travis, and parties at his
house on West 6th Street. At the University, Carter
supported my modern Persian literature program. I, in
turn, negotiated with the people in Comparative Literature
to make a coherent degree program out of his unfocused
earlier work, and thereafter took over as supervisor of his
dissertation committee.

I am vague about when his wife Judy left Austin for a li-
brarian's position in New Jersey, taking Sean with her.
Also I can't recall when Reza Baraheni came to speak,
although I do remember that, mostly for Carter's sake, I
gave him a glowing introduction at his afternoon academic presentation. At a panel that evening at which Kate
Millet and Babak Zahra'i also spoke, Baraheni's talk had
elements of high drama. He arrived with bodyguards and
spoke as if on a great and dangerous mission. People in the
audience shouted threats to his life. Several Iranian students turned on me and accused me of belonging to the
CIA. I looked over at Hasan Mahmudi, a basketball chum
from Mashhad who had come to Texas to study political
science, and asked him to put the students straight. Hasan
just stared at me.

I can put a date on another event, the December 1976
Modern Language Association meeting in New York.
Carter, Baraheni, and I attended East-West Literary
Relations Group sessions and had dinner one night at a
Wienerwald on Broadway or 7th Avenue. During dinner,
Baraheni, who often suggested to interlocutors that they
knew much less about Persian literature than he did,
stated that I had no business talking about English
literature either. I answered in kind, questioning the
qualifications of a Tabrizi whose degree in the subject was
from Istanbul and whose dissertation dealt with the
almost predictable subject of Khayyam and FitzGerald. It
is an all-time favorite topic for Iranian students abroad,
for example, Donné Raffat, Bahram Meghdadi, and
Parichehr Kasra, who do not refer to one another's work
or to the Persian sources. For that matter, 'Omar Khayyam
is hardly a major voice in Persian poetry. Sixty or seventy
unconnected quatrains, however pithy and anti-
establishment, cannot earn their author a prominent
niche in any poetic pantheon. Enough of this excrement, I
said, which brought dinner to an abrupt end. The next day,
Baraheni appeared at a panel where I was in the audience
and apologized. Given his robust ego which may come with
the territory in the case of his special genius, Carter must
have spent hours convincing him to compromise in this
situation. I appreciated the gesture. Not long after in
Boston, I gave a sympathetic talk on Baraheni called "A
Case Study of Politics and the Writer in Iran." Peter
Chelkowski came up afterwards and told me he liked it. I
hoped that Baraheni was treating Carter fairly. Carter was
giving, trusting and loyal, whereas in those days Baraheni
was self-serving and calculating. His latest book, a
personal and vaguely literary critical essay called *Kimiyâ
va khâk* [Alchemy and Earth] (1985), hints at a new
sensitivity in him. But personalities such as
Farrokhzad's, Golestan's, Âl-e Ahmad's, and Baraheni's
do not often mellow.

Durham, Monday, October 13th. This morning a thick
mist shrouded everything except the river. Walking to the
Oriental Library after breakfast, I couldn't see the
Cathedral towers and spire at all, Turner's painting thus
outdone. I stopped at the Centre to check the mail. Two
letters from Sorayya I read in my cozy Centre office I

somehow can't work in. There was nothing about Carter in the letters. That news wasn't written until the 8th or 9th. Elizabeth seems to be having a good time this term at St. Stephen's. I wrote her a paternal "smoking, drugs, and drinking beware" letter today just to let her know I am thinking about things. In the first grade, she heard from her teacher that smoking was bad for one's health, wisdom she brought home and hounded me with until I stopped smoking at midnight during Hafez and Jody Farmayan's 1976 New Year's Eve party.

In 1978, Hafez, who says he has never owned a television set, stopped by the house occasionally to watch interviews with Ruhollah Khomeini. He shared the excitement many of his contemporaries felt at the imminent end to the Pahlavi monarchy and at the prospect of new leadership with or around whom they might carry out the aims of the 1906 Constitution and recapture the spirit of the Mosaddeq years. At the time, I did not know what to think of Khomeini's statements from Paris, and had no clear picture of official Shi'ite attitudes toward Iranian national values and aspirations. Still, Khomeini's published vilifications of Jews and Baha'is were enough to persuade me that he personally promised nothing good for the likes of me in Iran. Coincidentally, I read Shahrokh Mescoub's *Melliyat va zabân* [Nationality and Language] (1982) at the Oriental Library this morning. Its sketch of pre-modern Shi'i attitudes toward Iranianness convinces me that secular-minded Iranians should have been fearful from the first rumblings in January 1978 about any turbaned figures in a post-Pahlavi Iranian state.

Hafez now talks with the tone of someone who will never see his birthplace again. For him, however, different sorts of separation from roots have constituted a life-long dynamics. He returned to Tehran in the late 1950s with a Ph.D. in Iranian history from Georgetown and made it to professor in short order at Tehran University. He also served as Director of Tehran University Press and supervisor of his family's library at the Faculty of Letters. In the mid-1960s, he gave all of that up and accepted a position as associate professor in the History Department at Texas, presumably to extricate himself from Farmânfarmâyân and Pahlavi webs.

Hafez may have never planned to return to Iran to live. But now that he cannot even dream about it, self-exile has become exile. He tells a story about his childhood that may have figured in his emigration to the States. His father named him after the fourteenth-century poet from Shiraz and insisted that he memorize *ghazals* by his namesake at a young age. Hafez recalls his terror when summoned in the afternoons by his father into the midst of gatherings of Iranian men and commanded to recite the latest memorized *ghazal*. It has been only recently, he says, that he has become able to look at Hafeian *ghazals* again. If only Hafez had interest in research writing or held non-Iranian views about biography, he might author a telling sketch of his family's history.

The only noise in the guest wing tonight is the chatter of the Indians. They say they are here to study census-mapping. Either it is too late for that in India, or it is one of the country's most relevant professions. The two of them talk alike, dress alike, eat mountains of non-meat things alike, and invariably come and go together.

The radiator is sputtering full blast and will shut off when the porter downstairs decides that that's enough for tonight. Part of me tonight wants a kerosene space heater and a basement room at Mashhad's University Club. "Those were the days, my friend," announced the Phillips 45-speed portable record player; and I thought, what ever can Mary Hopkins mean, "we thought they'd never end?"

Durham, Tuesday, October 14th. A sense of pattern and rhythm to life here soothed me today: breakfast at the Dining Hall, the walk along the river through town and up South Road to the Middle East Centre to pick up my mail, then over to the Oriental Library to work until two, and back to the centre of town for lunch, then back to my room and some writing, a jog or exercises, a bath, a glass of sherry, dinner at the Dining Hall, a stroll to the main library for an hour of reading, and a visit to the Half Moon Pub for a pint of lager, which I sip over a book of poems or letter-writing. As someone who ate *chelo kabâb* noon and night for almost nine months at Shamshiri's on Dâneshgâh Avenue in Mashhad, I can relish the expected.

Today had the unexpected as well: cheering letters from Sorayya and Elizabeth and lengthy chats with Dick Lawless at the Middle East Centre and with Reverend W.D.

Jones, Vice-Principal at Bede, who, upon my knocking on his office door, called out cheerily: "Qui est là?" I'll be lecturing on the LBJ Esfahan carpet on November 10th and on Âl-e Ahmad on November 13th for the Centre, and on the aesthetics of Persian carpets at the Senior Common Room at Bede on October 28th. Paul Luft has not yet scheduled the informal seminars on Ferdowsi and Farrokhzad I've volunteered to give to Persian program students.

Today was the first rainy day since I crossed the North Sea from the Hook of Holland on the 1st. It was misty and grey at eight and drizzling by nine. But the sky had cleared by the time I finished reading at the Oriental Library. Actually, I was researching an inconsequential and long overdue article for *The Encyclopaedia Iranica* on Herman Bicknell. At his death in 1875, Bicknell left behind a manuscript, which his brother Algernon published later the same year, with the title *Hafiz of Shiraz, Selections From His Poems*. Until Gertrude Bell's versions a generation later, Bicknell's now dated translations were what people in the know read. It is intriguing that this Englishman, one of many children of a self-made patron of the arts, began as a medical surgeon and ended up in Shiraz in 1869 thinking about Hafez. Some people credit him with having been the first undisguised Englishman to make the *hajj* pilgrimage to Mecca.

Durham, Wednesday, October 15th. Another letter in the post today from Sorayya, dated the 9th, describes how she learned of Carter's death from Lois after the call a week earlier from a friend saying that he was dying. Carter had apparently grown depressed a year or more ago and began to drink heavily. Four months ago, he started feeling unwell, but consulted physicians too late–he died of liver or kidney failure.

We met for the last time in San Francisco at the Middle Eastern Studies Association meeting in November 1984. Carter had just got tenure in the San Bernardino Valley school system and was relaxed. We decided at the conference reception to have dinner together afterwards. Bill Ochsenwald and one or two others joined us. Our first stop was at Carter's older brother's house, a stylishly decorated town house in a chic neighborhood. The brother was away, but had told Carter to help himself to his rack of vintage wines. Carter had me choose a bottle, an early

1970s' Medoc which we much enjoyed. Then we went to a nearby Italian restaurant and had an unforgettable dinner and time of it, all details forgotten. We laughed and carried on. Neither of us was in perfect form at nine the next morning when our panel began. I stayed up almost all night outlining a talk on Naderpour for it.

Carter didn't submit his Baraheni piece to *Sociology of the Iranian Writer* (1985), the volume planned for the panel papers. He felt that Baraheni's situation in Tehran was problematic enough without the further publicity of a review of his post-Pahlavi literary activities and views.

Approaching Dublin, Friday, October 17th. In the clear and still black sky, a full moon slightly to starboard hovers over the city. What looks to be an island, a largish mound, lies a bit more to starboard, and straight ahead is Dublin, studded with low lights like Mashhad seen from the plains in the distance. Are there no tall buildings in Dublin? Mashhad's tallest was four stories. I stood there smiling at the approaching city. But the wind on deck was much too strong and cold to tolerate for long.

After breakfast yesterday, I checked my mail downstairs. Just one letter, from Peter Avery with an invitation to speak at Cambridge on October 30th. I jogged, took a bath, and ate lunch at the Dining Hall. Then, with my things for the trip in my backpack and shoulder bag, I set out for the bus station. On the way, I mailed a xeroxed copy of the October 13th journal entry to Lois Bryant and letters to Hammy Dugan, George Meredith, George Shehan, and Frank Sheeran. The coach departed for Leeds in mid-afternoon. Just past Wetherby the driver had to turn around because he had forgotten to let off a passenger in the town, which has a lovely river and small waterfall. At Leeds, I raced up and down the outdoor, pedestrian shopper's mall and bought James Joyce's *Dubliners* and Avery's Penguin translation of Khayyamic poems to read on the boat. The Leeds-Liverpool ferry bus passed through Manchester, whose university looked new and grim. The coach stopped in Liverpool, then took us to the dock. The British and Irish Lines boat inched its way through a lock and set sail shortly before midnight. I celebrated with a pint of Guinness, roamed about, and finally settled into a slippery, plastic-covered, orange lounge chair. I slept fitfully, yet feel rested this morning, and am writing this

in the bar where an Irishman, with a build and voice like
Paul English's, is holding forth, cursing and swearing
about who knows what, to the delight of passengers with
no other show to watch.

* * *

Once off the boat, I took the coach from the B&I ferry
landing to Connolly Station and from there walked, as if
late for an appointment, to Daniel O'Connell Street.

O'Connell Street, O'Connell Bridge, the O'Connell monument. Mary Burch Tracy, whose older brother's middle
name was O'Connell, took pride in the Irish patriot as an
ancestor, pride contributing to her sense of being special.
On O'Connell Street I thought of ancestry and the meaning
it can give to things. I now cherish feeling connections
with my past, but hold it special only because it's mine.
Alex Haley's *Roots* first taught me that. As for Daniel
O'Connell, his street and bridge and monument are worthy
memorials to heartfelt living and self-made significance,
but also to failure, without which Irish-Americans could
not feel pride at being related to him. If the O'Connells had
succeeded in Irish history, there would have been little
reason for us Irish-Americans.

In that first hour in downtown Dublin, standing before
Daniel O'Connell's statue, my trips to Edinburgh last week
and to Hannover in September also came to mind. I got as
close to the Hillmanns as I ever expect to, driving with
Sarvar to two towns near Hannover. He took back roads
on the way back to Göttingen. We ate lunch at a roadside
restaurant near Leese and sipped mugs of a local brew.
Johann Friedrich Hillmann was born in Leese in July
1824 to a landowner called Johann Heinrich Hillmann
and a woman whose maiden name was Wichbrege or
Wieggrefe. Johann Friedrich's name appears only once in
German history, in a list of twenty-year old men eligible
for conscription in Hannover in the year 1844. His name
next appears in history as John Frederick Hillmann on a
citizenship application filed in the Marine Court, City of
New York, in 1846. He had sailed on the brig Republic from
Bremerhaven in December 1845 and arrived in New York
two months later. In his own autobiography, John
Frederick reveals that he had planned to take a ship to
Mexico and changed his mind at the last minute. In 1848
he married Merci Ann Burlew, who was born in 1828 to a
New Jersey family descended from Josiah Burlew, a

Revolutionary War soldier whose father Lewis Josiah
Buckalew was from Holland or Germany. Married in
Keyport before a Baptist preacher by the name of Wilson
Honsel, they had ten children, all born in New Jersey,
where John Frederick became a merchant. The second
child, John Henry, carrying on the family tradition of
naming the first-born male in alternate generations John
Frederick and John Henry, was the father of my father,
who was the fifth of eight children born to John Henry
and his Irish-American wife Mary Ann "Polly" O'Keefe.
My father's brother Harold, the only uncle I knew, named
his only child John Frederick, keeping alive the tradition,
because the oldest brother, Uncle Fred, had no male children. It is Cousin Fred who has given the rest of us
Hillmanns the story of how we got to the States in a two-
page report he mailed around the country several years
ago. It finally meant something that afternoon driving
back from Hannover to Göttingen. Leese taught me that I
have no special Hillmann feelings, but feel special for
bringing a journey full circle–this trip to Dublin
concludes it–and for being from somewhere specific. I'll
keep the second 'n' in Hillmann, but I belong exclusively
to the country my Craigs reached in the 1750s, my
Keatings perhaps a generation later, my Hillmanns in the
1840s, and my O'Keefes and Donegans a decade later. You
are where you are from, and the inevitable ties are
lifelong, at least as images in the mind's eye, where the
past is a dream you can see time and again, even when
awake if you wish. Yet, were Sorayya and Elizabeth here
with me today and were a job at Trinity College to
materialize tomorrow, we would call and think Dublin
home the day after.

Trinity College has wonderful ancient buildings around
lawn and cobblestone paths. A Henry Moore sculpture
rests on one quadrant of the lawn. I sat to write post cards
in the Art Centre, part of a complex of newer buildings in
stressed concrete and glass modernistically and styishly
flanking one side of the original Trinity yards. At the
university I visited the Long Room, stared at the two tiers
of pre-1800 books, and looked dutifully at the Book of
Kells. After also buying slides of Dublin from the College
Museum bookstore so as not to have to take pictures, I set
out for Daniel O'Connell again, this time on the north side
of the River Liffey. I located the Tourist Information

Organization, which reserved a bed and breakfast room for me at Miss E. Morgan's "Belmont" at 37 Hollybank Road in a neighborhood called Drumcondra. That turned out to be a fifteen-minute walk.

After lunching on a banana, a bagful of Irish scones, and a carton of skimmed milk in Belmont Room #5 while reading pamphlets I had picked up at the Tourist Office, I walked back down Parnell Street to O'Connell to see about a bus tour. The way seemed pleasantly familiar because I had just walked up it: crossing the bridge over the narrow canal with its little locks, walking under the train trestle, passing Georgian doors and inviting bars and many small businesses. I ducked into the General Post Office and touched the 1916 Easter Uprising Statue.

At the bus tour office they recommended a DART train to Bray down the coast. I could have got off at Sandcove to see the tower Joyce describes in *Ulysses*. But never having finished the book in several tries over the years, I stayed on the train and talked about Joyce with a genial young man next to me. The bay in Bray was beautiful, and the town a miniature, unspoilt Brighton, but mostly closed down till next summer. I walked along the sand-and-shingle beach, picked up a smooth stone for Elizabeth, and thought about oceans, especially the one which caresses Cape May three blocks from The Chalfonte Hotel.

Back in Dublin at dusk, loneliness and weariness visited simultaneously. So I did what any American should under the circumstances: read *The Herald Tribune* while munching a Big Mac and sucking a straw attached to a chocolate milkshake. On the walk back to the Belmont, I stopped at a neighborhood lounge for a pint of Guinness and a bag of peanuts. Everyone in the place knew each other.

As I looked at things today, including the Ha'penny metal bridge, the shops near Temple Market, Fred Hanna Bookstore, and the scene along the Liffey, my mind kept conjuring up thoughts of my own Irish ancestors, in the names of Keating, Donegan, Delay (or Dullea or DeLay), and O'Keefe, but without any sudden illumination. At the same time, Iran has faded into the very distant background. I realize that my reflections on Iran elucidate little about the human condition which might not more easily come from a sympathetic scrutiny of the Irish. I don't even plan to visit the Chester Beatty Library.

Dublin, Saturday, October 18th. Last night no later than ten o'clock and no more than three stories into *Dubliners*, I fell asleep. Ten hours later I awoke to faint sounds of rain on the roof. Miss Morgan's breakfast room pampered me with orange juice, corn flakes on which I sprinkled some of my private supply of bran, a fried egg, sausage, bacon, white toast served on a hot plate the crusts neatly trimmed off, orange marmalade, and a glass of milk.

Afterwards, the moment I stepped outside, the sun broke through the slate gray and remained out until I sat down at a restaurant table on Grafton Street at one. A drizzle resumed and continued while I consumed lunch and today's *Herald Tribune*. The sun reappeared once I started walking in the midst of a massive throng along Grafton. I turned down an alley and found Powerscourt Town House Centre, one of the pleasantest malls ever designed. In its center, under the bright skylight, a pianist plays the day's songs. A food court rings the second-floor balconies. I ate a piece of marble cake with whipped cream at a restaurant owned by a French woman. I bought two copper images from the *Book of Kells*: an eagle symbolizing St. John and a lion symbolizing St. Mark. Jim Bill's book on the Iranian Revolution will have "eagle" and "lion" in its title, for no good reason, even though lions and Iran have had associations for nearly three thousand years in many royal, religious, and cultural ways.

The morning was just as good: the walk downtown, a visit to the National Museum of Ireland and then an hour at the National Gallery. On my way to the museums, I stopped at Clery's on O'Connell Street, the city's largest department store, and bought a pair of navy-blue, fingerless wool mittens and an Irish check cap. I got almost teary-eyed at hearing Irish songs in the trinket and souvenir section. I also bought a sleeveless, wool V-necked sweater. I had wanted yellow, but pink was all they had in my size. So I settled for the pink and joked with the cashier that I will always think of the sweater as yellow. He smiled the way people in business do when a customer who must be tolerated says something stupid. All the while, I intermittently thought of Grandmother, who would have liked hearing about this Dublin excursion. My last purchase of the day was a red, baseball-style cap for jogging back in Durham.

The drizzle got steadier while I was looking at the very up-to-date exteriors of St. Patrick's and Christ Churches. So I hotfooted it to the bus station. After an hour of people-watching inside, which seemed colder than outdoors, I decided on a final Dublin entertainment: the nearest inviting restaurant, Liffey House, a short block away. Its ambience and decor featured paper napkins, dark-brown vinyl table cloths, and a husband-and-wife team not altogether happy (at least that evening). Photographs of the 1916 uprising and other events before Independence cover the walls. The creme of spinach soup, fresh crab, green salad, onion rings, a split bottle of a white Bordeaux, and I conversed and whiled away two hours.

Now almost two in the morning, the Connacht has not yet set sail, because of a gaping hole in its port side just above the waterline caused by contact–scuttlebutt has two versions–with either a pylon or another boat in the harbor. Repairs will take until mid-morning, say B&I staff on shore and on board. The bar can't open because we haven't set sail.

An Irishman from the country some forty miles outside of Dublin told me about growing up as one of five children and about emigrating years ago to England to find work. He had returned with his family to bury his mother who died at eighty-two.

I also talked to a former physical education instuctor from Gateshead who retired some years ago to an Irish village with only fourteen homes. She sold her car on Thursday and is going to England to buy another. Seated with her was a striking, plump young woman with a strange accent on her way to Wales, which is where her accent must be from.

From Dublin to Manchester, Sunday, October 19th. We are still hawsered to the Dublin Ferryport. I read and chuckled at Terry Butler's *Book of Bull* last night after conversations fizzled out and then slept in a lounge area until seven with a proverbial eye open for the adventure's next chapter. Awaking no worse for the wear, I accepted B&I's treat to breakfast, and am now expecting to transfer to another B&I boat set to sail for Holyhead at noon.

In other times and places, these past twenty-four hours would have been time wasted. At the moment, they seem purposeful, especially the business of my sweater. This morning when I saw the woman from Gateshead who wanted me to take cigarettes and wine for her through customs since I wasn't planning to use my duty-free privileges, she said that she had sent someone to look all over the boat for me. As she put it, she had told the person to look for a tall, thin, black-haired "young" man wearing a yellow sweater. I interrupted her at this point to have her repeat what she said about the sweater. She again said "Yellow sweater." I pointed to my pink sweater and told her that I had been wearing it since the previous afternoon and that I did not own a yellow sweater. She didn't believe me and was sure that she had seen me in a yellow sweater. I told her about the purchase at Clery's and my joking with the cashier that I would always think of the pink sweater I bought as yellow. We fell silent for some minutes.

* * *

In mid-morning I transferred myself to a boat called the Leinster. Having no gaping holes near the water line, it sailed for Holyhead at noon. During a complimentary lunch at a table with a porthole view of the sea and later on deck at the stern watching Ireland disappear, I tried to picture my ancestors as they watched its shores disappear when they set out for Boston and New York. What can have been going through the mind of my nine-year old Great-grandmother Ellen Delay?

I stood outside at the bow for almost an hour as we approached Wales, above it clouds and blue and sun seem etched into the sky, like a Matisse colorist paste-on or cut-out. We were off the Leinster at four.

On the train just before Bangor appeared mountains to the right and a beautiful river and cottages and homes to the left, and in front of them green fields and plump sheep. Wales is picturesque beyond my words. Luck got me rerouted here. Like the time I saw Beirut because I didn't have a re-entry visa from Istanbul to get back into Iran, and Pan Am had to put me up for a week while Iranian authorities in Beirut shuffled papers. What ever happened to the girl at St. George's Beach to whom I didn't have nerve enough to talk? And Karen Konig who comes to mind whenever I see a picture of Istanbul? That was 1966,

Beirut's last summer. Beirut seems far away and long ago. Iran would have as well today, were it not for a conversation with a sixtyish and portly expatriate lawyer and businessman, who regaled me (in Persian, to the consternation of nearby passengers on the train) with categorical castigations of Iranians left and right the whole way from Holyhead to York.

While we marvelled at the scenery, he poked fun at Iranians who wax nostalgic and hyperbolic about Iranian forests, rivers, gardens, and flowers, especially poets who describe the Iranian landscape as more beautiful than anywhere else. He said: "Just look at how green things are here. The same thing in the States, even in Washington, D.C. Can't these Iranians just enjoy the beauty around them and leave off exaggerating about Iran, which can't live up to their rhetoric?" He went on: "And they talk about life being better in Iran. When? Where? Whom are they hoodwinking, except for themselves? I'm not boring you, am I? When was life good in Iran and for whom? Every family has had children who didn't survive childhood. Every family has someone who has suffered in jail or who has died because of government action or negligence. If you ask me, Iran is good only for people who want to suffer to get their eternal reward on Judgement Day. The rest of us should wash our hands of the place and take our language and our poetry and our food and our love of family and friendship and our New Year's elsewhere. You're shaking your head? No, it's not treason or abandoning ship. After all, all of you Americans got to be American and then start acting patriotic by abandoning another country, your 'Iran,' only it was Italy or Ireland or Germany."

Durham, Monday, October 20th. On days like today, which is Jim's birthday, Iranians observe that "the sky's ass has been rent." Cold weather joined us from York northward last night. My itinerary by rail yesterday was: Holyhead (on Holy Island), across Anglesey (Island), Bangor, Colwyn Bay, Rhye, Chester, Manchester, Halifax, Leeds, and York, where we changed trains, and an hour there to enjoy its Victorian train station. Then came Northallerton, Darlington, and Durham by midnight. Everyone queued for taxis. I treated a student to a ride to a nearby college on our way to Hild-Bede.

They are good memories of Dublin and the journeys
across the Irish Sea, as well as Wales, the mountains
coming almost to the shore, sheep grazing almost to the
beach, narrow three-storied homes facing the sea, and the
vividness of the landscape in general. The images of
Dublin streets added much to *The Dubliners*, just as my
conversations in Austin with Sheraguime Youchidje
about Yush, and seeing pictures of the village and region
and Kiyomars Derambakhsh's documentary of the
Esfandiyari family home have added a world of textual
sense to Nima's poems, of his house, of rice paddies, of the
special solitude one can feel on one's own in the Iranian
north, of the mountains in the distance, and especially of
that gorge called "Mākholā," with its caves everyone
around thinks are haunted:

"Mākholā, the long river's defile,
goes who-knows-where
roars constantly
thrusts its body from rock to rock.
Just like a fugitive
(who does not seek the easy way),
it rushes to the downward slope
rushes to the upward incline
goes recklessly,
with dark night, like a lunatic with another lunatic.
It was going its way for a long time,
making links with many streams.
No one–for a long time now–pays it heed,
and it is busy with its mute singing.
It has fallen from the eyes of others
onto the lap of this ruin-like defile.
In its water's mute singing
"Mākholā" has a familiar message
and something to say about its manifest destination.
It goes but
like a stranger meeting a stranger
at every path it passes by.
It is going who-knows-where,
it roars constantly
to where it can empty into
like those driven from their homes.

Durham, Thursday, October 23rd. I got up late yesterday,
skipped breakfast, jogged, lunched at the Dining Hall, and
walked up the hill to the Oriental Library with a bounce in

my step. I talked briefly with Reza Navabpour and with Dick Davis and a friend of his who wrote her doctoral thesis at Swansea on English translations of Hafez. She told me that she had listed almost every known published translation, but had not come across my *Unity in the Ghazals of Hafez* (1976).

I walked back to town at dusk and found a table in the Manhattan Bar and a pint of Tuborg with my name on it. An hour later, I walked across Framwellgate Bridge and up North Durham Road to LaStalla for dinner. During it I wrote letters to Sorayya and Lois Bryant. Home before nine, I packed gifts for my return to Austin, wrapped a box of chocolates as a gift to the Bagleys who have invited me to lunch today, wrote a letter to Mother, and sat in bed reading Roy Mottahedeh's *The Mantle of the Prophet* (1985). He makes good use of Wells's thesis in his chapter on Âl-e Ahmad. The section on Avicenna is excellent, the material on Khayyam so-so. I learned a lot about how Shi'i clerics think through his depiction of an *âyatollâh*'s career. Or is it a composite sketch? There's something distant about Mottahedeh's work–is he a native speaker of Persian? The only woman in the book is Vita Sackville-West. No women figure at all in Mescoub's *Nationality and Language.*

Durham, Saturday, October 25th. At the University Library this afternoon, for no particular reason I pulled a copy of *Walden* off a shelf. I remembered hardly any of it from college. At that time, not knowing where Iran was, I wouldn't have noted Thoreau's mention of Sa'di's *Golestân* or the anecdote comparing cypress trees to free, independent, unencumbered men. I am all for "transacting some private business with the fewest obstacles." Not that I can accept Thoreau lock, stock and barrel–his Yankee fear of the flesh and comfort, his curious antipathy toward the railroad, or his implied preference of loons to the citizens of Concord. Of course, loons can be magical when you are twelve years old watching them dive into Quantabacook Pond, hand-in-hand with Carolyn Vickery.

Yesterday I didn't have much "spare time," a contradiction in terms Thoreau would say. I studied at The Oriental Library, attended a reception at the Centre, and then set out to the Davises for dinner. The walk itself was entrancing, up a winding, hillside road in the dark drizzle, with a

sudden new view of the Cathedral. I had a grand time at
dinner. Dick and his wife Afkham are good, friendly people who know how to entertain. Their house is full of
books, paintings and textiles, including a Fars lion rug
dated 1344. Reza and Farideh Navabpour were there, as
were Parvin and Glyn Pursglove, she the author of the
dissertation on Hafez translations and he a very agreeable
man and lecturer in English at Swansea. Another Iranian
couple joined us after dinner.

Durham, Monday, October 27th. Letters from Moh
Ghanoonparvar and Leonardo Âlishan arrived today.
Moh wants to stay on at Texas if Ali Jazayery goes on
leave next fall. Leonardo seems momentarily unfulfilled
in Salt Lake City, a city whose dry air and mountains in
the distance have a Tehran feel about them.

Moh and Leonardo, as different as any two peas from an
Iranian pod could be, showed up at my office door in
Austin in the mid-1970s wanting to use Persian in
Comparative Literature programs. Moh, ever easygoing,
America-loving, and quietly diligent, has since gravitated
toward literary translation. His versions of Ahmad
Shamlu's "Pariyâ" [The Fairies] and Chubak's *The Patient
Stone* show skill at finding parallel English folk voices
for colloquial Persian.

Leonardo is neither easy-going nor quietly diligent. He
is an intense romantic who insists on pursuing ideals
embodied in literary giants until the idol of the moment
crashes to the ground. At the same time, his bursts of
energy bookended by volatile reflecting have resulted in
stimulating poetry criticism. His "Tâhereh Saffârzâdeh:
From 'The Wasteland' to the Imam" (1982), "Ahmad
Shâmlu: The Rebel Poet in Search of an Audience" (1985),
and "Nâder Nâderpour: A Tiger in a Golden Cage" (1986) put
the three poets on the pedestals they have chosen for
themselves and then through sleight of pen remove the
pedestal, leaving readers with non-bardolatrous bases for
critical appreciation. In "Forugh Farrokhzad and the
Forsaken Earth," an essay he is writing for our
Farrokhzad Conference in Austin next February,
Leonardo reveals an exciting, broader dimension to his
critical vision. In it he engages myth, origins of culture,
notions of paradise, and culture-specific images of male
and female. He may be looking for personal myth-

ancestors, to find his own Armenian-Iranian significance in archetypes. He won't succeed in this venture any more than in his earlier romantic hope that poets might be better than other people. But his imaginative scouting into the distant Iranian mythological past to find food for contemporary poetic thought will offer readers a poignantly exciting trip.

Leonardo can do nothing about his immediate and practical concern, to make Salt Lake City more inspiring, to make it a poetic setting. He has to recognize that Persianists have to chose job over place if they mean to stay in the field. Moh recognizes that–he went to Charlottesville unquestioningly and would happily go to Tucson or return to Austin if a job materialized. I did the same when I came to Austin. As a Persianist I have to prefer teaching Persian here to doing anything else elsewhere.

As for Ali, he has been threatening to take early retirement, although I cannot imagine why. I'll stop teaching when I can enter classrooms only in a horizontal position. I've known Ali since the summer of '65 and still haven't the slightest idea of what makes this friendly and principled man tick. Once he retires, he may get out a book on Ahmad Kasravi. He was supposed to be at Kasravi's side the day in 1946 on which the latter was assassinated in Tehran. I once asked him if Kasravi's murder had anything to do with his decision to come to the States and thereafter not return to Iran to live. He replied that he had never thought of things in that light.

This afternoon I decided to skate at the Durham Ice Rink. In an almost dilapidated building, the almost deserted rink opened for its afternoon session at two, just as I arrived. I had a fun and uplifting skate for an hour. Even though my ankles were up to the task, my edges were unsure on turns, and my backwards skating was as jerky as ever. Circling counter-clockwise about an empty rink in silence seemed reminiscent of the whirling dervishes and as close as I'll likely get to their state.

Back at Hild-Bede, I have written an avuncular letter to Leonardo and a note to Three Continents Press about their footdragging on *A Lonely Woman.* The problem is probably money–3CP takes on projects which university presses should, but usually don't. I am in the middle of what Dad used to call a medicinal sherry.

Whitby, Wednesday, October 29th. I boarded the
Middlesbrough coach at ten this morning. The countryside from Durham to Stockton was green and clean.
Stockton's Wednesday market looked very busy, tents
lined up for blocks the way market stalls are in Vienna.
But Stockton and Middlesbrough themselves are by no
means quaint, with their smoke stacks and nuclear power
towers, and pollution on the horizon. The Middlesbrough
bus station is modern and in brick, with separate hall-
ways for each of twenty or more stands. After a change of
coaches came picturesque, sunny countyside, and then
glimpses of the North Sea. Sandsend appeared at the bot-
tom of a steep hill.

The end of the line was Whitby, a large town, about half
the size of Durham. It is home to a famous abbey in ruins,
a statue of Captain Cook, winding and hilly lanes, and
craft shops in hillsides around a harbor designed for
reproduction on post cards. Except for Debenham,
Woolworth's and Presto signs, nothing in Whitby offends
the eye. After a crab sandwich and a piece of homemade
pink-apple pie at the Circus Café, I strolled along the far
side of the harbor. I bought two pieces of orange and ginger
fudge, one I'm saving to eat while reading *The Times* on
the way back to Middlesbrough. I am writing this in the
bus station.

I also walked up the 199 steps to the Abbey. Should I
have remembered from freshman history class at Holy
Cross that there was a Synod of Whitby in 664? Not likely,
since I got a 'D' in the fall term and an 'F' in the spring. I
could never remember history until I got to Iran where it
was alive in the present. Now I can rattle off Iranian
dynasties the way Dad used to name English kings. The
abbey is delicate, finely wrought in stone, but just a
roofless skeleton now.

A hundred years from now these lines and pages will be
my skeleton, metaphorical, above ground, with a
manufactured spine. I remember in youth reading letters
by my great-grand-uncle Charles Augustus Craig to his
brother Horace in Searsmont from Montana, Washington,
and California. From 1851 to 1865, he kept promising to
send money and to return home himself. He never
imagined that he would be dead for a hundred years or that
a relative would cherish his letters then in Baltimore.

When Mother sold the Searsmont house in 1955, she held a jumble sale and auction. Things left over and Grandfather Craig's diaries she burned. Her rationale was that they were her father's private thoughts, including an entry on his last day, which he had spent reshingling May Brown's roof. He slept that night in the bed in which he had been born, and did not wake up. When I was younger, I was angry about the burning of the diaries for myself–I wanted to read them. It had taken him years to fill those uniform, bound volumes which I used to read on rainy summer days as a child to learn things about Mother and Grandmother. But I now feel sad for David Craig himself whose voice has thus not reached the present. Mother did keep Mabel Moore's books, which Grandfather Craig had inherited from Mabel's mother, his Aunt Mary Keating Moore Livermore of New Hampshire.

Keswick, Friday, October 31st. I'll fall asleep tonight reading Wordsworth in anticipation of my pilgrimage to Dove Cottage in the morning. Matthew Arnold complained about Wordsworth that he could have been a better poet had he read more books. Is that true? Should not the better poet be the person skilled at poetry who lives more life in life than in books? If T.S. Eliot had lived more exuberantly or if Hafez had not not worked as a convention-bound court poet, I might have even better poems to read at night. But then Hedayat did almost all of his living in his mind and in conversation with books, and there is much "poetry" in *The Blind Owl*.

Today has been as carefree and sparkling as days get. The sunny bus ride from Newcastle to Carlisle was glorious: patchwork green fields and hills, neat stone villages, several sizable towns–Corbridge was one–and proud, solitary farm houses every kilometer or so.

The Lanes at Carlisle is a stylish shopping center, and the Cathedral yet another beautiful church. After a walk around town, I wolfed down a salmon-and-cucumber sandwich and a scone and boarded a local bus for Cockermouth. I there walked down the eighteenth-century Main Street and at Fletcher's bought a sleeveless, green, nylon hunter's vest. On a bridge between Main Street and Wordsworth's birthplace, I marvelled at how the River Cocker races through town. It dawned on me that the slobbering, affectionate dogs Aunt Mercy always had in tow got their name from the town. Other names also came to mind which I hadn't thought about since English classes at Creighton–Annette Vallon, Robert Southey, and Dorothy Wordsworth, and the group that flocked to Wordsworth at Keswick. The house in Cockermouth where he was born is almost grand.

The local bus to Keswick passed Bassenthwaite Lake, as beautiful a lake as there is, long and narrow, sheep grazing at its green bank, on the other side strangely colored mountains, a few sailboats moored in the water, utterly peaceful, framed by autumn foliage.

In Keswick, I've a miniscule, third-floor room under the eaves at the Bridgedale Guest Cottage on Main Street, several blocks down from Town Centre, which is chock full of tourist shops that somehow belong there. A dozen of them sell woollen and leather goods and hiking paraphernalia. Half the people on the streets are dressed for serious walking and hiking and have determined, yet contented looks on their faces, many blotched by the air. The lake side of town has rows of enchanting, dark, multi-storied homes facing a golf course and a public foot path to the lake.

Durham, Saturday, November 1st. The last leg of my Lakeland excursion was a train from Newcastle, there being no night coaches from there to here. I had set out for Newcastle by way of Penrith in midafternoon. From north of Keswick, the view of the mountains, some snow-covered, was breathtaking, but then outdone by the panoramic vista from the switchbacks snaking up the mountains to Alston. Behind our Wright Brothers coach stretched 180 degrees of mountains, an orange sun setting above Grasmere, now forty kilometers away to the southwest, as if Wordsworth wanted to enlighten me further.

Grasmere was the day's first adventure. I boarded the Ribble Bus at nine. The drive was spectacular from my perch on the upper deck. I watched mountain tops hold up the sky and rivulets define slopes and cascade down to rivers. Unheeding ducks went about their business. The other people on the bus, dressed in anoraks and boots, seemed expectant, set to join the elements at whichever town they had picked to get off. They spoke little and may have been hiding a shared secret, their Thoreauian knowledge that "a taste for the beautiful is most cultivated out of doors, where there is no house and no housekeeper."

Actually Grasmere wasn't my first adventure. Happy to be half-awake all night with the splatter of rain on my garret roof, I ate breakfast early, paid my b&b bill of £6.50, and walked to Keswick Lake. It was glassy and peaceful, orange and red and rust along the shores and trees mirrored upside down on the water, nothing tarnished. The lake on the way to Grasmere was the same. Keswick itself, approached from north or south, is as inviting as a town could be.

Dove Cottage, its history, and its environs have me born-again believing in nature's beauty, long walks, the healthiest possible food, indifference to fads and things, and nurturing a feel for art, for poetry, either creating it or responding to it. For some moments there, I felt on the verge of intuiting the true and inexpressible relationship between art and nature: "I have learned / to look on nature . . . hearing oftentimes / The still, sad music of humanity, / Nor harsh nor grating, though of ample power / To chasten and subdue."

Dinner kept me company last night at Keswick's Cottage Restaurant. I exchanged pleasantries with a pint of Jenning's Bitters, gossiped with potato and leek soup, got serious over grilled Borrowdale trout with almonds, a baked potato and peas, and reminisced with a glass of port afterwards. I read my Penguin Wordsworth throughout, and every so often smiled at my sense of well-being.

From the moment the bus departed Newcastle on Thursday until it grew dark near Hexrow tonight, I felt tranquil and inspired. I sat in Wordsworth's chair in the upper front room at Dove Cottage. Standing at the window, despite more recent building on the far side of the lane, I could see the lake, just as he did seated and writing. Altogether the journey spanned a mere hundred miles. Yet the other end was another world, with people whose accents reminded me of Mainers. Dove Cottage had the wooden, musty smell of Grandmother's house.

Durham, Monday, November 3rd. During my Ferdowsi lecture this afternoon at the Oriental School Annex before nine witnesses, I heard myself testifying to strong convictions about values expressed in literary works. It was my first talk in years outside of class or a conference, on a literary subject of my own choosing. I believe in Sohrab's aims. In his martial and monarchical age, he set

out to establish himself as an equal to his own father and
to replace a hereditary king with his father, whom he
considered (wrongly it turns out) more worthy to be king.
Iran has needed such a revolutionary view ever since the
Sasanids established their dictatorial, patriarchal rule
over that sad, despairing land in 224 C.E.

After the lecture, some of which he dozed through, came
an evening of conversation with Mr. Bagley. I asked him
to choose a restaurant. He drove us to Ramside Hall (or
some such name) on the Sunderland Highway three miles
northeast of Bede. We had a cocktail sherry, then the game
casserole of rabbit and quail, with carrots and courgettes
on the side, and cheesecake for dessert. Mr. Bagley
analyzed the Iran-Iraq war and reminisced with first-
hand descriptions of Khuzestan, Baghdad, Karbala, and
Najaf. A Côtes du Rhone Villages 1984 joined in the
conversation. Crème de Grand Marnier on the rocks ended
it all. Five hours of talk, none of it about money, vaca-
tions, America, jobs, or the weather. Mr. Bagley's
understanding of Iran is intense and personal. Indeed, he
is opinionated, but his interest in the culture is heart-
deep, sincere, and unromantic. He has been in things
Middle Eastern at least since a trip in 1943. Retired from
the Durham faculty in 1981, he spends much of his time
translating, mostly for *The Encyclopaedia Iranica*. He has
translated Badrolmoluk Bamdad's *From Darkness into
Light: Women's Emancipation in Iran* (1977) and Ali
Dashti's *Bist-o seh sâl* [Twenty-three Years: A Study of the
Prophetic Career of Mohammad] (1985) as a favor to the
author.

By the end of the evening, as a consequence of repeated
puffings on his pipe, he was coughing and wheezing. He
occasionally breathed as loudly as Dad did once
emphysema took hold. I almost said something. It was
enjoyable and relaxing to be out on the town with someone
who knows things I want to hear.

Durham, Friday, November 7th. The coach stopped first at
Ferryhill, then at Newton Aycliffe, and lastly at
Darlington. I sipped a cup of hot chocolate at the depot
cafeteria there and boarded another coach for Barnard
Castle. On the way, it stopped at several places, among
them "Staindrop." The River Tees meandered along with

us. One town displayed a plaque which read: "Durham County Tidy Town Award."

I walked up and down the main street of Barnard Castle, looked at the namesake pile of walled stones and round tower. With all its grand history, perhaps not a single castle stands in all Iran. I bought a country pasty and a carton of orange juice, which I stuffed into my backpack for the next leg of my United Auto Explorer Excursion.

That was the bus for Bishop Auckland. It passed through Cockfield where huts stand mute watch over ravaged, gray-black hills turned inside out in the search for coal. Back in Durham by mid-afternoon, I have since busied myself with Khaqani's "Ode on the Palace at Ctesiphon" for hours that have slipped by without notice.

Take care, o heedful heart, to mind the eye:
see Ctesiphon as a mirror of admonition.
Along the Tigris, stop at Ctesiphon,
and let a second Tigris flow onto Ctesiphon's soil . . .
Weep anew for the Tigris and give it your eyes' alms,
even though the shore takes alms from the Tigris . . .
Once the palace chain at Ctesiphon broke,
the Tigris went awry and twisted like a chain.
From time to time call out in the tongue of tears
to hear with the heart's ear the palace's reply.
Each battlement gives advice time and again;
heed advice from those heights in your heart's depths:
You are of earth, and we now the earth beneath your feet;
trod upon us, and scatter two or three tears . . .
This injustice befell us, the court of justice;
what privation must await palaces of the unjust?. . .
Do you laugh at my eyes that they weep here?
O, weeping is for eyes not weeping here.
This is the palace where from imprints of faces
the threshold dirt became a portrait-gallery wall.
This is the royal court where Babylon's king
was just a slave, and Turkestan's Shah a doorman.
This is the same splendid pavilion where
the lion woven into the tapestry would attack Leo.
Imagine it is that age: with your mind's eye
see the court's chain, the throng in the square.
Dismount, put your face to the chess-cloth ground,
see No'mân checkmated under the Sasanid elephant's foot.
No, rather see the No'mân-like, elephant-slaying Shahs
trampled by the elephants of night and day.
Many an elephant-slaying Shah a chess elephant trapped,

checkmated by fate on the square of hopelessness.
The earth is drunk, having imbibed, instead of wine,
Anusharvan's heart's blood from Hormoz's skull.
Counsel enough was visible then on his crown,
a hundred pieces of advice now hidden in his head.
Sasanid kings, their glory and their gold
are gone with the wind, become one with dust . . .
O Khâqâni, beg counsel from this palace door
so that henceforth the Khâqân will beg at yours.
If today a vagabond seeks provisions from the Sultan,
tomorrow the Sultan will seek provisions at his door.
If Meccan goods serve cities along the way,
take a travel gift from Ctesiphon for Sharvân.
From Mecca come prayer-beads of Hamza's clay,
so you take beads of Salmân's clay from here.
Don't leave this sea without a drink.
One mustn't leave this sea unquenched . . .

Khaqani here arguably voices one of the deepest,
culture-specific themes in all of Persian literature: the
incomprehensibly cruel fact that Iran's grandest moments
have almost always been in the past, that Iranians can
always think they are living after their time. The poetic
speaker hears the Sasanid ruins say to him and through
him to us: "Yes, why do you marvel that in the world's
meadows / owls follow nightingales, and lamentation
song?" As a Craig-Keating-Donegan-O'Keefe-Hillmann
American, I have no such feelings about my past,
although, as I grow older, I am better learning personal
dimensions of the feeling in "thinking of the days that are
no more." They sometimes do seem, as Tennyson put it,
almost "Deep as first love, and wild with all regret." As for
this day, it was visually resonant and otherwise quiet.

Rex and Cheris Smith had me to dinner at High Table at
St. Aidan's last night. We gulped a hasty sherry
beforehand in the Senior Common Room where the Lord
Mayor seemed weighed down by the shining medallion on
a chain around his neck. We had beef Stroganoff and
claret for dinner, and then drinks back at the Senior
Common Room. I talked a lot during dinner and enjoyed a
conversation with a Mrs. Shirawi from Bahrein. Her
husband, a cabinet minister, is watching their three
children back home.

Durham, Saturday, November 8th. Basho describes the beginning of a day like this well: "On a snowy morning / I ate
by myself / chewing tough strips / of dried salmon."
(Noberyuki Yuasa's translation from *The Narrow Road to
the Deep North*, Penguin, 1975). On the walk downtown,
facing a day without conversation, I wondered what would
be the point to anything I might do during the day. At the
Town Hall, I forced myself to examine the crafts displays
one-by-one, until the rhythm of the fair got to me. The
Town Hall grand room is lovely. The handicrafts were
mostly sturdy and useful. I almost bought a shoulder bag
for Sorayya. Then I walked, shop to shop, throughout the
town, ending up at the public library, shivering because I
had forgotten to put my hunter's vest under my jacket. At
the library, I read *The Guardian.*

An editorial supporting the Iraqi combatants in the
Gulf war made little sense. England and America should
learn to do nothing about Iran and let the situation work
itself out, which it eventually will with no decisive
outcome if the history of southern Iraq and Iranian
Khuzestan repeats itself. After all, the dramatic outcome
happened in the seventh century when the Arabs attacked
Iran and changed it forever, bringing "false lights,"
according to Akhavan-e Sales, in place of the true light of
earlier Zoroastrian culture.

While in Marks and Spencer's, I heard drums. I rushed
outside to see a drum and fife corps and others clad in
green march up Silver Street, playing tunes and chanting,
"I, I, I, R, A!" I felt goose bumps. They were serious and
mostly very young, redfaced people who believe passion-
ately in something. The believing itself makes Belfast and
Khuzestan comparable.

"Home" at four; still with nothing to do, I rewrote part of
my Hafez chapter for *Iranian Culture*. I feel as close to
Hafez as to any pre-modern, non-Western poet, but not
that close. His confidence that life has a plan, a reassuring
divine plan, and that he can discern the good and the
better, creates a gap between us. I have travelled to his
world and can accept it while on the trip, but he could
never visit mine. Bicknell was not far off in observing
that the bard from Shiraz was the most joyous poet
imaginable. Hafez had unshakable confidence in how
things will turn out, even with his troubled dark nights of
the soul, soul-felt separation from the perfect object of

affection, and his sense of deeply rooted hypocrisy in much human activity:

> From the world's garden, one flower-face is enough for me.
> The shadow of that strutting cypress is enough for me.
> Away from all the deceitful people of the world,
> the large, bitter wine cup is enough for me.
> Although the palace of paradise is the reward for good deeds,
> a Magian monastery is enough for a libertine beggar, like me.
> Sit at the stream's edge and see the passage of life;
> this sign from the transient world is enough for me.
> Look at the world's bazaar and the suffering in it:
> This profit and loss, if not enough for you, is enough for me.
> For God's sake, don't send me from your door to heaven;
> for of all being and place, your neighborhood is enough for me.
> Hafez, complaints about the inclination of fate are unfair.
> Flowing talent and flowing *ghazals* are enough for me.

Durham, Tuesday, November 11th. My Persian carpet slide talk at Elvet Riverside tonight was fun. In the audience of forty people I recognized a dozen faces. Click. Mohammad Reza Pahlavi and Lyndon Baines Johnson strolling across the White House lawn. Click. The Esfahan arabesque medallion carpet which then Prime Minister Amir Abbas Hovayda presented to the Johnsons. Click. Click. The carpet, Royal Square images, Safavid medallion designs, and *shâh 'abbâsi* motifs. Click. Its atypical royal blue background color. Click. MRP wanted to communicate royal confidence and values to LBJ. Click. Modern flowers added by the designer don't fit in. Click. A scene of the Revolution, proof that Pahlavi modernization didn't fit in. Click. Click. Wait a minute, look at the religious images in the carpet. Too bad MRP and LBJ didn't recognize those images and didn't notice that the modern flowers didn't fit in. Thank you. Questions followed. An anthropologist objected sensibly to my thesis. But my pictures were a speech, not an academic piece.

Then came dinner at the Centre. Reza and Farideh Navabpour and Dick Lawless arranged it. One guest by the name of Maxwell Frye sported epaulets of dandruff on his double-breasted, brass-buttoned, blue blazer and called Ebrahim Golestan's house in Bolney an "atrocious" re-make of a sevententh-century chateau. He and his wife Jane Drew say Golestan told them he had to flee Iran after

Asrâr-e ganj dar darreh-ye jenni [Secrets of the Treasure of the Haunted Valley] (1974).

Durham, Wednesday, November 12th. After a serene day at the Oriental Library, I walked to Pizzaland on Silver Street for supper. Seated at my table, nose in *Time Magazine*, I suddenly sensed that someone was sitting down opposite me. The person said nothing. I looked up, prepared to be indignant. It was Dick Davis. We talked and then walked to his house. I drank homemade beer and talked with his mother-in-law visiting from Tehran. Dick first went to Tehran to teach. He chanced there to meet Afkham. They have two girls, Mehri and Maryam, the latter named after Afkham's younger sister who died young. Dick's colloquial Persian is good, but he doesn't seem eager to use it with everyone.

It has never occurred to me to ask Iranians what they think of my Persian. With neither a perfect ear nor photographic memory, I learned the everyday side of the language quickly enough, but still don't usually prefer to use it instead of English in serious conversation, except in a knock-down, drag-out. Then I love Persian and say things I wouldn't dare say in English, black and white, categorical pronouncements that would sound outlandish to me in English and perhaps offensive to others. Because Iranians expect to hear outlandish things from an American speaking their language, they seem not to take offense.

Dick gave me copies of his *Seeing the World* (1980) and *The Covenant* (1984). I had read all three of his collections–the third is called *In the Distance* (1975)–in early October, right after first meeting him. He is a skillful versifier with views on poetry close to those of Iranian traditionalists. He no doubt thinks Nima and Farrokhzad mediocre poets, because they subordinate meter to the word-world they try to create. Ahmad Shamlu would not qualify as a poet in compositions lacking meter.

Dick has a poem called "A Letter to Omar," which he composed shortly after leaving Iran in 1980. In it he reviews his acquaintance from childhood with Khayyam, first through Edward FitzGerald. Three stanzas have special appeal and relevance (*The Covenant*, Anvil House Poetry, 1984):

You left the busy trivia unspoken:
Haunted by vacancy, you saw unbroken
Miles of moonlight–time and the desert edge.
The high-walled gardens, man's minute, brief token.

Such fierce uncertainty and such precision!
That fateful metre mated with a vision
Of such persuasive doubt . . . grandeur was your
Decisive statement of our indecision.

The warring creeds still rage–each knows it's wholly right
And welcomes ways to wage the martyrs' holy fight;
You might not know the names of some new sects
But, as old, the nation is bled slowly white.

Durham, Friday, November 14th. During my Âl-e Ahmad
talk last evening. Paul Luft appeared amused at several
points, as I went far beyond where he would suppose the
evidence allowed. Sooner or later, I've got to write that
book on Âl-e Ahmad–his life seems so full of perennial
Iranian contradictions and tensions. He needed Islam, but
may not have believed in God. He resented the West, yet
modelled himself on Western social protest writers and
other oppositionist intellectuals. He prized individuality,
yet was unable to accept Forugh Farrokhzad, the most exciting individual of his age. He adopted the dervish manner, yet envied affluent contemporaries. He decried patriarchal politics, yet cultivated a following himself among
younger writers. He strove to be a modern man of the
present, yet was almost devastated by being unable to
father a child.

Afterwards, Paul and Reza joined me for dinner at
Ramside Hall. I had duck, Côtes du Rhone, and a napoléon
for dessert. It was a cheery evening, although Reza's cheer
has limits any more. He thinks constantly about the dim
prospects in Persian studies and about Iran's even dimmer
prospects. He may belong in Iran, as do most of my academic Iranian acquaintances. I may even belong there. Yet
what life would our children have there? Sons eligible for
the military draft? Daughters becoming women? Wives
who are equal partners in public here?

As for Paul, I get the implication, reading between the
lines of what he says, that German scholars, closer to the
Orient, understand Iranians and things Persian better

than the English and the Americans. Illustrative of that scholarship is Annemarie Schimmel's essay on "Hafiz and His Contemporaries" (1979), reprinted in the just-published sixth volume of *The Cambridge History of Iran* (1986). Here are its opening and closing paragraphs:

> One of the great experiences in Iran is a visit to . . . the delightful garden that is laid out around the tomb of Hafiz . . . and to open the Divan-i Hafiz to look for a *fa'l*, an augury. . . During such a moment the visitor may perhaps recall the beautiful lines written by the "last classical poet" of Turkey, Yahya Kemal Beyatli (1881-1958), who uses one of Hafiz's central concepts, that of *rind* ("vagrant"), in his poem "Rindlerin ölümü."

> Perhaps only a poet can fully understand the secret of Hafiz's poetry–as Goethe certainly did. Therefore we owe the best explanation of Hafiz's poetry to Rückert, the Orientalist-poet, who sings in truly Hafizian style of the double-sided fabric of Hafiz's colourful lines in which sensual and supra-sensual experience are intricately woven together. . . "Where Hafiz's mere words seem supra-sensory, he speaks of the sensual; or does he speak, where he seems to speak of the sensual, only of the supra-sensory? His secret is un-supersensory [i.e., not beyond sense-perception], because his sensual[ity] is supra-sensory."

Behruz Neirami called from London yesterday after lunch. He saw Sorayya last week in Austin and may turn up at the airport tonight.

Gatwick, Saturday, November 15th. With the whirr of a floor polisher in the background, I am seated carefree and wide-eyed in front of the Country Cafeteria on Gatwick's second level, just down the hall from where Elizabeth and I bought orange juice and visited the post office on June 11th on our way to New Haven, a night's rest, the ferry, and on to Paris. The cafeteria opens for breakfast in another hour.

Behruz was searching the terminal for me when I arrived at nine, a half-hour late. The coach got caught in a traffic jam on the M1 near Luton. After Heathrow, the bus driver, who had begun his day in Newcastle thirteen hours earlier, seemed disorientated. I helped him find Gatwick. I also chatted with a member of the English National Golf team on the way to a friendly match with Spain. He has hopes of becoming famous, but is now on the dole.

Behruz treated me to supper. We talked until after midnight. As upbeat as ever, he landed feet first after the Revolution. Mandana and Nazi live in an apartment in West Hempstead, while he spends about two-thirds of his time in Tehran dealing in books. He may have had something to do with organizing Al-Hoda Bookstore on Charing Cross. Behruz's attitude is the exception. For while I am having warm thoughts about flying home, about having a home to fly to, almost all of my Iranian acquaintances behave as if in exile. However they left Iran, and for whatever reason, and even if it happened long before 1979, they now see their native land as no longer near enough to what it was to think of it as home still. I am starting to get hungry. Where is breakfast? And what about me? Will I get to Iran again?

As relished as breakfast will be, it won't taste better than breakfasts at Mashhad's University Club. Hamid Âsudeh would rap on my basement door at seven, walk to my table hands full (as I opened my eyes and remembered in half-amazement where I was), and set down a half-slab of *tâftun* bread, a three-*riyâl* crock of yoghurt, a chunk of Bulgarian white cheese and a small mound of jam in wax paper, and a pint bottle of milk. The Mashhad milk pasteurization plant had opened just months earlier, in the spring of 1965. I'd get up and eat, forgetting again that the jam would drip from the bread on to my hand, the while marvelling at the Persian language Hamid and I conversed in, at the strange outside beyond my window, and at the myriad possibilities the Mashhad day was about to offer.

The sociologist and social reformer Ali Shari'ati (1933-1977) and
I at Sorayya's house in Mashhad in June 1967. Ali had joined the
Sociology Department at Mashhad University the previous fall.
He took part in English classes which fellow PCV Doug Fossek
and I set up for colleagues who had thoughts of conducting
research or teaching someday in the States. Anti-Pahlavi
Iranians called Shari'ati's sudden death at forty-six in England
political assassination. Many people also consider his writings
influential in the success of the Iranian Revolution. In the spring
of 1980, the Islamic Republic of Iran honored Shari'ati with a
commemorative postage stamp, the only postage stamp issued
since the Revolution picturing a man in a necktie.

Peace Corps colleague Michael Jerald and I in the Mashhad
bazaar in front of a painted scene of the Shi'ite shrine to Emâm
Rezâ in March 1971. Before taking the picture, the photographer
needed assurances that Mike was sympathetic enough to Islam
to appear in a photograph with such a holy backdrop. Of
Ruhollah Khomeini's actions after returning to Iran, the most
surprising to me was something he did not do. Not once in the
ten years before his death did he visit Emam Reza's shrine.

Prominent Persianist Heshmat Moayyad and the poet Ahmad Shamlu at our house in Austin in April 1977. After dinner that evening we prevailed upon Shanlu to recite poetry. He began with his most famous work, the folk-poem called "Pariyâ" [The Fairies] (1956). Shamlu's reading entranced even guests who did not know Persian.

The writer Sadeq Chubak and Sorayya at our flat on London's Mecklenburgh Square in April 1982. After publication of his novel called *Sang-e sabur* [The Patient Stone] (1966), Chubak "retired" from creative writing, something I have always found puzzling about his career and that of several other *engagé* Iranian writers.

Shams Âl-e Ahmad and I in the library at his house in Tehran in December 1989. His *Az cheshm-e barâdar* [From a Brother's Eyes] (1990) may stimulate further biographical inquiry into the life of his older brother Jalâl Âl-e Ahmad (1923-1969), the most influential social critic and essayist in the Iranian 1960s.

My niece and nephew Yashar and Sara Abbasian in front of the Tehran Museum of Modern Art in December 1989. The statue of the woman behind them has had leggings and a scarf added after the establishment of the Islamic Republic of Iran in April 1979. Official concerns about women in public and male-imposed rules about women's dress are the most startling aspect of Iranian society today for an American visitor who knew Iran before 1979. Who can have much hope for societies where men legislate behavior for women?

Sadeq Hedayat's sister Akhtarolmoluk Hedayat, her daughter Mehrangiz Dowlatshahi, and I at their apartment in Paris in January 1990. One purpose of my visit, which Jaleh Violet arranged, was to get family permission to organize a conference at The University of Texas called "Sadeq Hedayat and Persian Literature." Held in January 1991, the conference drew nearly twenty-five speakers to Austin, among them: Mashallah Ajoudani, Leonardo Alishan, Michael Beard, Hamid Dabashi, Derayeh Derakhshesh, M.R. Ghanoonparvar, Simin Karimi, Homayoun Katouzian, Jalal Matini, Hamid Naficy, Azar Nafisi, Mahmoud Omidsalar, Nasrin Rahimieh, and Ehsan Yarshater. Hedayat relative Dariush Dolatshahi entertained conference participants one evening with *târ* and *seh'târ* music and a satirical Hedayatesque monologue.

Part 2
Tehran

Tehran, Monday, December 11th. From my hotel room
window at the crack of dawn, I took two snapshots. From
the misty distance, somewhere in the park next to the hotel, came the cadenced chant of marching soldiers. Sounds
of motor scooters, motor cycles, pickup trucks, cars, and
trucks grew progressively louder and filled peaceful spaces
of quiet.

I rode the elevator down to the lobby, walked toward an
upholstered bench by a pillar to the side of the main entrance, and sat down, intending to take in the scene.

Lâleh International Hotel used to be called the Tehran
Intercontinental Hotel. It is located on Doctor Fâtemi
Street, which used to be Âryâmehr Street, and set in the
north end of Lâleh Park, which used to be Farah Park. The
hotel has the air of former royal status about it. The
formerly glittering cocktail lounge with its long, formerly
sleek, sunken bar is now a breakfast room and sandwich
shop, the bar sinks used for washing dishes, flatware,
cups, and glasses. The lobby's wall-to-wall carpeting has
an indefinable tired color. Signs abound of efforts to keep
things up. But gray-brown tinges have invaded the furniture and the walls. Fresh paint covers the hotel's exterior
stucco façade, some splattered on the bushes and ground.
Desk clerks, busboys, taxi clerks, and other staff are polite
but harried, and wary of the mostly foreign guests. Near
the front revolving doors, a bearded man in a drab grey
suit sits at a table behind a sign reading "Security." In the
early morning, small groups of foreigners, none speaking
Persian and many speaking just passable English, mill
about the lobby, waiting for drivers or Iranian coworkers
to whisk them away to work sites, offices, and ministries.
Koreans, Japanese, Germans, French, and English, but no
Americans. Artfully crafted metal letters on the far wall
behind the tea serving area read: "Down with the U.S.A." A
not-yet-open snack shop advertises "pistachious." Twenty
years ago Iran was often truly pistachious. A Mozaffarian
handicrafts shop is the chief lobby business. The day Eliza
was born, I bought a silver vase from Mozaffarian's on

Takht-e Jamshid Street to take, full of flowers, to
Sorayya's bedside at Alborz Hospital.

At seven-thirty, I set out for Parvin E'tesâmi Street, just
two blocks east of the hotel. By now, the traffic was heavy
enough to remind me of how dangerous crossing Tehran
thoroughfares used to be. When I couldn't find No. 15, the
owner of the neighborhood dry cleaner's asked me who I
was looking for. I said, Mr. Abbasian. He pointed to the
building three doors down, No. 10. I had confused a hand-
written Arabic zero with a five (but luckily not in print in
a scholarly publication, and the dry cleaner won't tell
anyone).

Yashar and Sara were up and getting ready for school.
Maliheh was just putting dishes on the table. Abbas, she
said, was still in Dubai. I told her that he had called
Sorayya in Austin on the 8th and sounded under the
weather. We sat down to breakfast: Tehran-style *tâftun*
bread with butter, white cheese, and quince jam, along
with hot tea. The jam dripped off the bread on to my palm
just like it used to. Sara said little during the meal, but
sent friendly messages through sidelong glances. Yashar
warmed up to his American uncle right away. He brought
an empty wallet to the table as evidence for his mother of
his need for pocket money. I quickly gave him ten *tomans*.
By lunch time he had spent all of it, on a single ball-point
pen. I should have given him a hundred *tomans*. Money is
worth less than a tenth of what it was when I was last here.

After a visit to the brother of a friend to check on
money and a quick taxi ride back to the airport to pick up
my passport, I was back at Maliheh's for lunch with her
and the children. Their schools have half-day shifts.
Homework takes up some of the afternoon. I'm not sure
what they do after that.

After lunch, I walked to Vali'ahd Square, where they
used to display the prizes for the Wednesday lottery,
Paykân automobiles, sometimes filled with money. Of
course, its name is not "Crown Prince Square" any more,
but rather Vali'asr [guardian of the age]. In the early days
of the Revolution, it was called Mosaddeq Square, a name
I could live with. Mike and Julie Jerald lived just off the
square. Varzandeh used to play the *santur* at the King's
Hotel bar nearby. Sorayya and I had dinner occasionally
at the Baccarat Nightclub just north of the square, mainly

to see Gougoush perform. Farhad sang "Jom'eh" [Friday]
on one of those evenings. Our favorite restaurant, for a
time, was Quartier Latin on Kâkh Avenue a little south of
the square. Two blocks east was a basement nightclub
where Sorayya and I spent New Year's Eve in 1969 marvelling at the more-Catholic-than-the-Pope anticipation and
celebration on the part of frenzied Persian-speaking rev-
ellers.

I hailed a cab heading north and peered out the window
trying to find a personal past in a surrealistic present. The
buildings were as strange and as familiar as Hedayat's ge-
ometric structures in *The Blind Owl.* At the corner of
Abbâsâbâd I looked east to catch a glimpse of Shahr-e
Farang Cinema where Sorayya and I attended the First
Tehran Film Festival in 1970. Behruz Vosuqi sat next to
us at one session, but we didn't know him then. His *Dâsh
âkol* won first prize. *Gâv* [The Cow] got second prize.
Showhar-e âhu khânom [Âhu Khânom's Husband] came
in third. Works of prose fiction were behind all three.

My taxi passed by the high-rise buildings at Vanak
Square, the Chattanooga Restaurant which used to feature
semi-nude chorus girls in the postprandial floor show, the
Miami Nightclub, the Safavi Bazaar with that restaurant
which ordered two dozen *mafreshes* from us at Caravan
Carpets, and the most obvious landmark, the Royal
Tehran Hilton Hotel. Its opening in 1962 had filled
Mohammad Reza Shah Pahlavi with sufficient pride to
have him issue a commemorative postage stamp for it.
Sorayya and I ate dinner there only once or twice, but
liked it on occasional Friday afternoons for its *café glacé.*
We passed the little park called Sâ'i which often appeared
as the setting for lovers' strolls and trysts in Iranian
movies. New, abstract and ironically oppressive names
are everywhere: Independence, Freedom, Revolution. In
the old days, places had equally discomfiting royal family
names: Pahlavi Square, Pahlavi Avenue, Pahlavi
Foundation, Farah this, Crown Prince that, Reza everything else. To send a piece of mail anywhere you had to
lick the backside of a stamp with the face of Mohammad
Reza Pahlavi on the front.

Back at the hotel by dark, I ate a chicken kabob dinner
alone while a middle-aged Iranian man talked to himself
and gestured emphatically at a nearby table. Since return-

ing to my room at eight, I have been writing and listening
to Ali Akbar Hashemi Rafsanjani talk about his recent
visit to Khuzestân. A desk clerk just called to ask me to
turn the volume of the television set down. Europeans in
the next room had complained about the noise. As I listened to Rafsanjani, I wondered what American news
commentators could mean by characterizing any turbaned Shi'i cleric as a moderate politician or statesman.

Today is not eventful in the telling, although my eyes,
ears, and memory tell me otherwise. Of course, I have left
out the real event, the reception accorded me last night at
Mehrâbâd Airport, where it took me two hours to clear
customs and passport control. What first struck me about
that scene was an irony: most of my fellow passengers who
had been serious, even glum in the waiting area at
Frankfurt, ran from the buses to the Mehrâbâd terminal
building, unable to resist getting ahead of others and taking care of quickly what they seemed hours earlier not
happy to do. In contrast, as eager as I was to get into
Tehran, I walked slowly toward passport control lines.

Once my turn came, the all-business, blue-uniformed,
moustached passport official announced my obligation as
an American to change $300 cash on the spot at the offi-
cial rate. $300 was the total amount of cash I had brought
with me, but not for cashing at the official rate at the airport. I planned to buy *riyâls* with it at ten times that rate
on the street. So I protested the regulation and avowed that
I had only $250 in cash. Bargaining couldn't hurt, I
thought. The passport official matter-of-factly replied
that in that case I would have to board the next Lufthansa
flight back to Frankfurt. Caught in a verbal trap of my
own making, insofar as I could not now suddenly produce
$300 whereas only moments before I had owned up to only
$250, I persisted in bargaining, knowing that I'd end up
paying $300.

The passport official told me to take a seat until he had
finished with everyone else. Meanwhile, officialdom had
become aware of the Persian-speaking American in the
area. So when a German businessman who spoke no
Persian protested his just-lapsed visa and imminent de-
portation, the passport people asked me politely to serve
as their translator. It dawned on me that the old Tehran
persisted in the new: the about-to-be-deported American

arrival would become a trusted interpreter for the similarly situated and now perhaps suspicious German.

By this time, a second official, a tall young man clad in an American army field jacket, approached and asked to examine my luggage. I opened my locked suitcase, duffle bag, and backpack. The tall young man looked at everything carefully while he politely asked questions. The conversation about my obligation to change money at the official rate continued.

A third official then appeared, shuffling along in slippers, wearing tired polyester slacks and sporting three or four days' growth of beard. As he drew near, the tall young man advised me that this third official would ask the same questions he had, but with more serious things on his mind. I smiled and said that my answers would stay the same regardless of the seriousness of the questioning, whatever that could mean.

The third official inspected my luggage again and jotted down names of addressees on letters Sorayya had given me to mail from Tehran. He expressed surprise on hearing that I didn't know all of the addressees. He wondered about the plastic bottle in which Sorayya had poured a supply of wheat bran and marvelled at seeing so much equipment for the mouth: toothbrush, toothpaste, mouthwash, dental floss, throat lozenges, and Certs. He promised to look after my things while I went upstairs to the passport office to leave my passport until I returned later in the day with $300 cash to exchange.

While talking to the police upstairs, I felt invigorated and in control of a situation not at all in my control. Back at the lower level, the third official asked me about my religion. This is not an easy question. I became a nominal Moslem in 1967 in order to marry Sorayya. I tell him I am a Moslem. He asks me if I pray. I say I do not because I am my own *mojtahed* and choose not to pray. I add that the late Âyatollâh Milani had tacitly approved my approach to Islam and that I have documentation to that effect (his seal on a letter which Ali Shari'ati had helped me compose). Four or five onlookers seem impressed. The questioner lapses into silence, fingering his *tasbih* beads.

I can leave the passport area now. Questioner #2 volunteers to take me to the Lâleh Hotel, a surprising turn of events which does not surprise me. He hails a cab, pays for it when we reach the hotel, and introduces me to the hotel staff in the lobby. All of them know him. He then reads my telephone message from Gertrude Nye Dorry and jots down her number. He accompanies me to Room 1117, looks it over, and watches me unpack. Ten minutes later, he pulls out a wad of Iranian currency the size of a thick delicatessen sandwich, offering me as much as I want, no strings attached. I decline with effusive thanks. He gives me a card on which he has written his name and telephone number, and leaves. I then began a vigil until dawn, thinking that I had passed a sort of muster.

On Saturday afternoon, when I looked back down the ramp to wave goodbye to Sorayya at Houston International Airport, this Tehran trip momentarily seemed a bad idea. I was wrong. It was a great idea, even if, as Steinbeck warns readers in *Travels with Charlie*, the trip has already begun to take me, rather than me take it.

Tehran, Tuesday, December 12th. Today I walked up and down memory lanes. From the hotel, I set out west on Doctor Fâtemi Street to Amirâbâd Street, and paid the Iran Carpet Museum a quick visit. Nearly one hundred twenty finely woven carpets of varied provenance, from classical antiques to products of the 1970s, hang on pipe frames or are spread out on sunken floor spaces. No other museum in the world rivals its display, not Room 42 at the Victoria and Albert, not the Metropolitan, and not Vienna's Folk Art Museum. Ironically intriguing about the permanent exhibition is the importance given to court-produced or otherwise royal carpets with explicit royal themes. Erwin Gans-Ruedin's *Splendor of Persian Carpets* (1978) gives a decent sampling of the collection, but doesn't communicate the monumental impressiveness of the actual carpets underfoot. At least twenty carpets exhibit portraits of mythological and historical royal personages. The Islamic Republic has here decided against rewriting history or implementing a monolithic censorship, two serious excesses of the Pahlavi monarchy.

Just south of the carpet museum on Amirabad lies a government handicrafts bazaar. Its kiosks and other small buildings display ceramic wares, leather goods, textiles, glass, paintings, and other handcrafted goods. Standing by the ledge of a waist-high window at one shop,

a man with a cigarette dangling from his lips was desulto-
rily weaving a Kurdish *gelim*. Apparently, only flatweave
carpets get exported these days. Almost all the men here
smoke cigarettes.

Beyond the handicrafts bazaar southward stands the
Tehran Museum of Modern Art. On the outside its mod-
ernistic lines in stressed concrete and statue-filled
grounds are none the worse for Revolutionary wear. I left
it for a rainy day and walked through part of Lâleh Park,
picking up Amirabad at the main park entrance on what
used to be called (Queen) Elizabeth Boulevard.

Farther down Amirabad, I decided on a shoe shine. A
conversation got going right way. He has had the shop, a
corner location, for forty-nine years and wouldn't know
what to do with himself if he didn't work or if he had to
work for someone else. A sparkle in his eyes, quickness
still in his gnarled hands, and Âzarbâyjâni straightfor-
wardness in his Persian, he wet and lathered and rubbed
and polished and wiped and otherwise gave my walking
shoes a treat and a treatment. We gradually agreed on a
price of thirty-five *tomans* during the conversation. Also
during it, another customer came in, a woman who fid-
geted with her *châdor* and talked down to my Tabrizi
friend. "Are my shoes ready?" "Which shoes, Madam?"
"The black patent leather high heels I brought in last
week." "No, not yet Madam, perhaps tomorrow." "What's
taking so long? And, by the way, how much will I have to
pay?" "100 tomans." "But you said 75 tomans when I
brought them in." The old man lowered the boom as he
turned to me and smiled: "If you knew the price, Madam,
why did you ask?" She left in a huff. He knew it would be a
happy day. He may have had lots of them over the years. It
has never been easy to be one's own man in Iran. My
Tabrizi friend figured out a way when he bought his little
shop not long before the Russians and the British occupied
Tehran and sent Reza Shah Pahlavi packing.

Two blocks farther south, I reached what used to be
called 24th of Esfand Square. A sea of men, out of work
and grim, milled and roared in waves about the square. I
turned onto Shâhrezâ Avenue, which also has another
name now. I walked passed the building which used to
house the Capri Cinema. Sorayya and I attended the opening of *The Cow* there twenty years ago. Everyone buzzed

with excitement that evening. Sa'edi's screenplay and
Daryush Mehrju'i's direction had given us what we then
thought was a daring, if oblique and symbolic, critique of
Pahlavi society. I walked past the University. The brick
troughs and spigots next to the street, for use by the faith-
ful before Friday community prayers on the university
grounds, were disconcerting enough so that I opted against
a stroll through the campus where I had spent graduate-
student parts of days for three years.

I continued down Shâhrezâ to Hâfez Street. A traffic
bridge now hovers over the intersection. I looked up to the
second floor windows of the former offices of our Academy
of Language. The building was much the worse for wear
and had none of the freshness and promise of 1973 on it
any more. A faint outline of the Persian letters for *mak-
tab-e zabân* was still visible in the window at the second-
floor landing. The sounds of our Persian and English
classes and my daily rush with partner Behruz Neirami to
get lessons ready flashed through my mind. One Saturday
morning in January 1973, after having wined and dined a
SAVAK official at Shekufeh Now Cabaret two nights earlier to arrange for a private school permit at the last
minute, Behruz and I opened the doors to nearly 140 students, mostly Iranians hoping English would open doors
for them and some foreigners expecting Persian to help
them make sense of the strange place they were getting ex-
tra pay to live in. We typed and mimeographed lessons day
by day, wolfed down Moby Dick cheeseburgers for lunch at
our desks, and shared spoken dreams of being better than
everyone else in town and unspoken dreams of making it
big.

I backtracked to Kâkh Avenue and walked up it to
Kucheh-ye Giv, a block south of where the Israeli Embassy
used to be, before it turned into the offices for the Palestine
Liberation Organization. Before Giv Alley, on my left, is
what used to be called Shâh Rezâ Bakery. Now called simply Reza Bakery, it sells little more than bread. But the
name change is food for thought: take the Shah out and
what's left is (Emam) Reza.

Our second floor apartment at No.12 still has our signature on it in the form of the window screens which
Sorayya insisted that the Peace Corps install. I stood
across the alley and gazed at those windows, wanting to

sink into reverie about our life there, trying to evoke images of Eliza's first steps and sentences, of our joyous New Year's parties and the excitement of being near the literary scene. Hushang Golshiri's masterful *Prince Ehtejâb*, the silence in the print media after Âl-e Ahmad's death, Sa'edi's *Gur va gahvâreh* [Grave and Cradle], which I managed to buy from the publisher before the government banned it, Mohammad Hoquqi's *She'r-e now az âghâz tâ emruz* [New Poetry from the Beginning until Today] (1972), conversations with Sadeq Chubak, socializing with Iraj Afshar, the Iranology conferences in Tehran and Shiraz, and my own exchange of articles on orientalism with Baraheni in *Ferdowsi* stand out in memory.

My last stop before a siesta at the hotel was Kâkh Square. The florist shop and *âbgust* café are still there, as is the girls' high school. However, on the school's courtyard wall a bold and multicolored hand-painted sign now reads: "eslâm bâ khun roshd kard" [Islam grew/spread with blood]. No. 65 Takht-e Jamshid Street, then Peace Corps headquarters and now a company building, seems much as it was twenty-five years ago. Standing across the street and seeing the tops of the same evergreens in the front courtyard that surrounded the pool in which some Volunteers cooled off after hot bus rides from the provinces, I could almost feel again the excitement we young people shared as we came and went great distances to jobs then important to us. I could almost taste the Pepsi Colas in bottles Reza would bring along with tall glasses full of chopped ice.

Jeeps and Wagoneers caked with dust and dirt from Birjand and Khoy, Bandar Abbas and Bandar Pahlavi, would fill the courtyard. Ghassem Zarrin would be rushing to the airport to help a Volunteer who had lost this or that through Customs. Arakel Baroyan would be smoothing out ruffled Embassy feathers. John Newton would be recalling his ten days in Khorâsân attending to earthquake victims near Tabas and Ferdows. Don Croll would be talking in his perfect Kermân accent to an official at the Ministry of Education. In the early 1970s, Mike Jerald and I would excuse ourselves from the office to sneak down to Ferdowsi Street to price carpets and study their designs.

Tehran, Wednesday, December 13th. I lugged my bags from the hotel to Maliheh's apartment at dawn this morning and was seated at the dining room table before Yashar and Sara were up. They appeared at seven, but were not in a hurry, even though Sara had to be in line in her school's courtyard by 7:15 and Yashar in his at 7:30. Maliheh served them hot milk which Yashar wouldn't drink until his mother skimmed the skin off the top. She then prepared tidbits for Sara, small pieces of *tâftun* bread with a dab of butter and strawberry jam on each. For Yashar she rolled up larger pieces of bread on which she had spread butter, white cheese, and jam. Maliheh worried about the time, whether both children had put everything into their bookbags, and how careful they'd be walking to school, Sara just across the street and Yashar down Fâtemi Street to Martyr Raja'i Elementary School for Boys across from the Hotel Lâleh.

Sara left the table quietly, went to the living room where she had brought her school things, and put on a grey *maqna'eh*, a cowl-like covering which left only her face visible, ears, hair, neck, and shoulders now hidden. Maliheh stuffed a snack into Sara's bookbag for recess. Sara was now visibly eager to get to school. But Yashar, a year older and in the third grade, dawdled at the table. He was perhaps thinking that waiting to the last second to leave for school would bring the pleasure that sometimes comes with risk-taking. Perhaps he was offering a little challenge to the system which prescribes the shaving of his head every few weeks and proscribes wearing the American blue jeans which Sorayya and I send him.

Sara bid her mother a quiet, quick goodbye and was moments later standing at curbside below, but hesitant to cross the street by herself. Maliheh picked up a *châdor* and left the apartment in her slippers with the *châdor* draped over her head and body. She took Sara's hand and led her across the street. Sara ducked through the metal gate and disappeared behind the tall brick wall around the school courtyard. The noise of the girls in the courtyard was cheerful and loud. Everyone was in a hurry to say hello, talk about what they'd done since yesterday, and worry about homework assignments. The principal began to speak into a microphone from the school porch. The chattering of the girls stopped.

Meanwhile, Yashar had found his shoes, which he tried
to put on without untying the laces left tied when he had
taken them off last night. He donned a blue laboratory-
type coat, the boys' uniform, and over that put on a parka
still a size too large for him. He hurried out the door to cut
through an alley almost at a run to make it to school just
at the bell. Maliheh worried more about him and the traffic in the alley and on Fâtemi Street. She then sat down at
the table for a cup of tea and several of the tidbits which
Sara had not eaten.

From Sara's school yard came the high-pitched voices
of the girls in unison, praising God, praising Khomeini,
damning America, quoting from the Koran. I listened and
wondered what effect twenty minutes of daily school-yard
recitation was having on the Saras standing there hooded
and docile.

From Maliheh's I walked eastward on Fâtemi to
Pahlavi and up to Abbâsâbâd and up Vozarâ to Iran
University Press to meet with Nasrollah Pourjavady. We
talked for three hours. He is full of ideas, energy, and will.
For him Hâfez is a Sufî, period. His collaboration with
Peter Lamborn Wilson called *The Drunken Universe: An
Anthology of Persian Sufi Poetry* (1987) interprets
Hâfezian wine as lacking alcoholic content. He is skepti-
cal about what America produces and stands for and has
the self-assurance of a believer who has paid his dues.

Afterwards, I took a taxi to Tajrish Square, which
teemed with people, buses, minibuses, cars, pickup trucks,
and hawkers. I walked down Maqsud Beg Street to
Zamineh Bookshop. From there Karim Emami and I
strolled over to the Old Shemirân Road, now called Doctor
Shari'ati, where we lunched at a small, almost elegant
kabob restaurant. On the way, we passed the riverbed
which had flooded two summers earlier, drowning hundreds, if not thousands, of people. We talked more back at
Zamineh until four.

From Tajrish, I took a minibus for three *tomans* down
to Elizabeth Boulevard–it took an hour to get there–and
then walked down Karim Khân Zand Street to the new location of Nashr-e Morgh-e Âmin Bookstore to leave a
message for Reza Baraheni. A police lieutenant from
whom I asked directions asked me where I was from. I

said, "From that country, you know the one." He smiled, saluted smartly, clicked his heels, and wished me well.

It turns out that a Texas graduate named Ebrahim Rahimi who took my Modern Persian Poetry course years ago manages Morgh-e Âmin. His six-year-old son Nima had a confident English "Hello, how are you?" for me. It echoed scores of wide-eyed "hálo meéster"s from the 1960s.

Whatever poetic heritage Nima Yushij has left for the future may even pale in comparison with the popularity of his given name, which he gave to himself as a young man. I know a dozen children named Nima, first and foremost my own wonderful nephew in Göttingen. It is a name which proclaims that neither Arab Islam nor Persian monarchical tradition need be the corner stone of one's Iranianness. People tell me a government office now advises people on the appropriateness of names presented for birth certificate registration. In the late 1920s, at the beginning of the Pahlavi Era, the government forced Iranians to choose Western-style surnames.

Outdoors, walking along busy streets, I have yet to see any foreigners, except for Afghans and the occasional Arab. The lobby at the Marmar Hotel, which has single rooms for 200 *toman*s a night, was full of Arabs this afternoon. People passing by stare momentarily and evidence recognition of my foreignness. But they move along, do not turn around, and thus draw no undue attention to me. High-school students find my backpack amusing. One yelled after me yesterday, "What grade are you in?" Every so often, someone hazards a "Guten Tag," perhaps hoping I am German and not from that other country. Young married couples hold hands while strolling along uptown streets. Teenage girls in groups smile and talk excitedly about things. They crowd little shops examining, but not buying, make-up, eyeshadow, and lipstick while covered with cloth from head to foot. Only their brightly colored shoes, even athletic hightops, announce their individuality. Older people do not have smiles on their faces. Many people are in a hurry, and the vehicular traffic keeps them on edge. Long lines of people wait for buses everywhere.

Sorayya sounded next door on the telephone this morning when I called her from the telephone company on my way to Iran University Press. I argued with an operator

who was taking much longer than the promised thirty
minutes to connect me with Austin. Other customers, who
were accepting the delays in sullen silence, looked quizzi-
cally at me as I asked about the delay. The noise in the
room was exciting: "Zanjân, Hello. Hamadân, wait a
minute. Call through to Shirâz. " I remembered the telephone sequences in Mas'ud Kimiya'i's *Bâgh-e sangestân*
[The Stone Garden]. "Cabin 6, *emrikâ, âqâ-ye hilman.*"

Tehran, Thursday, December 14th. Shams Âl-e Ahmad,
still young in eye but otherwise looking every one of his
sixty years, moves gingerly because of a chronic back
problem. Stting on the edge of a make-shift bed in his library, he sips what looks like water from a glass full of ice
and smokes cigarettes in a holder one after another. The
room exudes warmth, the walls covered with metal book-
cases, one large section devoted to a collection of his
brother's works and another with multiple copies of those
works.

Shams talks in a rich voice that I hope sounds like
Jalal's for the sake of hearing the latter after death.
Shams is comfortable and dutiful as the younger brother.
It is his lot and part of his profession. He also has self-
confidence of his own. He has a son named after Jalal,
born a year after his famous uncle's death. Shams warms
up the minute he senses sympathy and frankness. He rel-
ishes the possibility that our conversations are politically
sensitive, while I know that they are not. Because he likely
knows little about literary biography, he may not understand how useful he can be. Everything he relates in two
and a half hours is interesting, but none of it new to me,
except for his recollections about Jalal and Simin's brief
separation in 1964 on account of Jalal's revelations in
Sangi bar guri [A Stone on a Grave], which remained unpublished until 1981. Most of what he tells me appears in
his forthcoming book called *Az cheshm-e barâdar* [From a
Brother's Eyes], which he showed me in manuscript.

Who were Jalal's best friends in the 1960s, I ask.
Manuchehr Hezarkhâni, Eslam Kazemiyeh, and Hushang
Vaziri, all ten years or so younger and all then bent on
wielding more than pens in reforming Pahlavi Iran. Jalal
told Shams that Sa'edi was a two-party Turk, that is to
say, both Marxist and Nationalist. Shams says that he

and Parviz Shapur are good friends. He probably wonders
why I care about all of this, about Tehran literary currents
in the 1960s. About his own writing and Jalal's, Shams
says, "We don't do research. We come from a religious family, so we pronounce edicts."

Many secular-minded intellectuals blame Jalal for the
Revolution. One piece of evidence for them is the Âl-e
Ahmad commemorative stamp which the Islamic
Republic issued in the fall of 1988. Would that writing
other than the Koran could so influence behavior here.
Those who don't blame him ridicule him and question his
independence from the system. Ebrahim Golestan looked
down his nose at Âl-e Ahmad while he made films under
contract with the Iranian monarchy, one of them on the
crown jewels. He later sold his film studio to the government. Faint praise on my part for Âl-e Ahmad 's candor
and doggedness over dinner one night in Austin raised
Nader Naderpour's ire to the point that I had to keep quiet
or dinner would have ended in a shouting match.
Naderpour worked for the Iranian National Radio and
Television Organization and produced his first politically
conscious poetry only in the aftermath of the Revolution.
In *Nationality and Language*, Shahrokh Mescoub charac-
terizes Âl-e Ahmad's writing "on the complicated and mul-
tifaceted subject of 'weststruckness' [*gharbzadegi*] as superficial and hasty, and derived from political biases and
from behind ideological glasses which necessarily offered
preconceived views." In the Pahlavi era, Mescoub worried
about contemporary social ills and the superficiality of
engagé analyses of those ills while he worked for the
Iranian Tourist Organization and the Plan Organization
and wrote sympathetically about Ferdowsi's *Book of
Kings*, a panegyric epic of Iranian kingship.

Meanwhile Âl-e Ahmad had plugged away as a Persian
teacher, wrote and worried about his culture, went as far
as censorship would allow in criticizing the political status quo, and defined at least one Iranian malaise for a
whole generation. His Persian prose may be the most distinctive authorial voice since Sa'di's *Golestân* (1258). The
new Texas Advanced Modern Persian Prose Syllabus,
which Aziz Atai is developing, will raise eyebrows when
Persianists see that we base half of our third-year Persian
course on *A Stone on a Grave.*

Not that Âl-e Ahmad was altogether likable or a scholar. His analyses of history and the West are jaundiced. He exaggerated in his social criticism. His polemic style gets on my nerves. But he was not a superficial intellectual or writer. He mattered and matters still. The tryptich of *Weststruckness, Lost in the Crowd,* and *A Stone on a Grave* are milestones in Persian literary history and Iranian thought in their bold depictions and analyses of his senses of rootlessness, godlessness, and childlessness. Âl-e Ahmad took admirable risks in making his own flawed self a cultural issue.

Tehran, Friday, December 15th. I have felt inexplicably at ease from the moment I stepped into the A2 waiting lounge at the Frankfurt airport. The lounge was full of Iranians and a dozen or so Europeans who sat somewhat apart. In my larger classes at Texas, American and Iranian students usually end up in clusters separate from each other. I was the only American there and am perhaps the only American male on his own in hotels or on the streets here at the moment. There is at least one other American male in town for sure: Jon Pattis, a telecommunications engineer from Aiken, South Carolina, whom the Islamic Republic sentenced three years ago to ten years in prison for spying.

Nevertheless, on long walks each day, in taxicabs riding to and from appointments, in offices and homes, nothing has seemed bizarre except for talk about domestic politics. Having no reason to go south of Tehran University or the Ferdowsi carpet shops, I have not seen any mullahs or public displays of religiosity, even praying. Oppositionists allege that because Shi'i clerics fear for their lives no clerical turbans or cloaks appear on the streets.

To be sure, anti-American slogans grace walls along streets and in hotel lobbies, and women cover themselves with a variety of scarves, shawls, long coats, and dark stockings. But even that seems visually familiar because of media exposure and because of similar custom in such provincial areas as Mashhad twenty-five years ago. Writers still have their sense of mission and seriousness. Bookstores are pulsing with intellectualism. The traffic noises which start almost at dawn, hurrying crowds of people walking along main streets in the early evenings, long lines at bus stops and taxi stands, the sidewalk vendors and hawkers, and the great variety in Persian accents are as I remembered them.

As for differences, shop fronts have taped Xs on their plate glass windows and doors to protect against shattering during Iraqi missile attacks. Signs every couple of blocks direct people to underground bomb shelters. Because of terrorist threats, postal clerks repack all packages to be sent anywhere in Iran. Only children, who are oblivious and trusting, and teenagers, who feel immortal and full of promise, do a lot of smiling in public. Underemployed men line the streets hawking single *vinestón* cigarettes. No women appear in public places where men congregate, except in the long lines for foodstuffs at stores which sell things at special prices for people with coupons.

Up at six this morning, I wrote letters to Sorayya and Elizabeth before breakfast. Yashar got himself in gear early too, once he realized I had no plans for the day. We went shopping for stamps and a toy and walked for almost two hours with no luck. Even Tambr-e Sinâ was closed. Because the owner has bad eyesight, he has me write down and add up the prices of stamps I choose. I give myself the bill and then pay him.

When I suggested to Yashar a look-see at the Iran Carpet Museum, he said okay. His readiness to accept looking at carpets as real fun saddened me. We watched the master weaver there work for a while. He has been weaving the same medallion carpet for nine years, a finely woven, Turkish knotted, 6'x9' piece with a complicated field of vines and *shâh 'abbâsi* motifs. He slits the yarn, pulls forward two warps, inserts the yarn, and repeats the process effortlessly and mindlessly, taking care of colors one at a time across a row as defined on the cartoon pinned onto the loom just above his head. He responded in a thick Âzarbâyjâni accent to our questions.

We then walked leisurely around the room. Yashar read each carpet description and looked up at the carpets to see if somehow what was announced as from Kermân reminded him of Kerman. He liked the portrait carpets best of all, especially a monumental compartment carpet from Tabriz depicting Rostam's *Shâhnâmeh* exploits. (It's on page 192 of *The Splendor of Persian Carpets*.) If not the quintessential example of what Donald Wilber calls "The Triumph of Bad Taste: Persian Pictorial Rugs" (1979), it comes close. But I won't tell Yashar that.

Back in the rain on Fâtemi Street and not yet ready to go home, we followed my umbrella to the Lâleh Hotel. We gave the Mozaffarian shop a once-over. While Yashar looked at knives, I got distracted by a group of Frenchmen lording it over Mr. Mozaffarian, whose French wasn't up to neutralizing their patronizing banter and bargaining. We then walked across the lobby to the Yaddi Gallery. Yashar looked at coins and more knives while I talked with the owner. I also looked at Sasanid coins. Joel Hettger had given me notes on things to look for. But the shopkeeper interested me more. Speaking Persian with a native Tehran accent, he said he had been leasing the same location in the hotel for seventeen years. All of the Ferdowsi people, he told me, have emigrated to Haifa, Tel Aviv, New York, and Los Angeles. But Jews, he said, have not suffered harassment since the Revolution, nor have Armenians. He did not mention Baha'is. Criminals get punished, he said, not Jews. He added, "My customers know goods, so I can offer only good things at fair prices. Glad to see an American here finally." In response, as Yashar and I left for tea and a piece of cake in the lobby, I said, "Glad to be an American here finally." We ate our cake underneath the "Down with the USA" sign. I bought a bag of candy for Sara.

Back at the apartment, our wet shoes and socks off, we are sipping cups of hot chocolate. The rest of the day promises reading, more writing, a game of chess, and a popular Japanese serial on television about a woman who has raised a family by herself. Now her son wants to marry someone she disapproves of. Over the years, I've met three Iranian mothers who came to Austin to rescue sons from American fiancées and wives.

Tehran, Saturday, December 16th. My day began with a walk across Fâtemi and down Pahlavi to Karim Khân Zand Avenue to see an exhibition of sculpture by Lilit Terayan at Kânun-e Nashr-e Noqreh Bookstore. Then came a search for the third edition of Baha'oddin Khorramshahi's *Hâfeznâmeh* there and at Cheshmeh, and Morgh-e Âmin. It will be out next week. Then I walked

along Roosevelt Avenue, part of it a giant pit where they
are excavating the chief subway line from above ground.
Lunch with Gertrude followed at Nâyeb Chelokabâbi on
Pahlavi north of Takht-e Tâvus. She drove us in her
Volkswagen Beetle through traffic I wouldn't challenge
even in a video arcade game. We had barley soup, *dugh,* yoghurt, *tâftun* bread, and rice and lamb kabob. While eating, Gertrude kept on a buttoned-up gray raincoat and a
scarf over her head tied at the chin. In that get-up, she
seemed about to leave the table at any moment.

The rest of the afternoon and part of the evening I spent
at No. 16 Arz Cul-de-sac off Bizhan Lane in Tajrish with
Simin Daneshvar, five hours of listening to warm-
hearted, animated, maternal, serious talk on Farrokhzad,
Shamlu, Golestan, Baraheni, herself, and the ever-present
and forever absent husband Jalal.

A report I cited in the introduction to John Green's
translation of *Lost in the Crowd* (1985) that Shamlu had
retracted or denied his dedication to Âl-e Ahmad of his
poem called "Mard-e rowshan" [Bright Man] had irritated
Daneshvar. She said she confronted Shamlu with it. He
denied ever even thinking such a thing. Of course,
Daneshvar doesn't know that Sa'edi told me during a conversation at his Gallieni apartment in July 1984 that Âl-e
Ahmad never meant that much to him and certainly never
was his mentor.

Nothing has changed in the in-fighting among the modernist literati. Daneshvar, Baraheni, and Shams Âl-e
Ahmad continue to trade accusations and different versions of events. The most recent chapter is Baraheni's six-
teen-page, open letter to Shams. But the most interesting
is Najaf Darybandari's interview in *Donyâ-ye sokhân,*
which Azar Nafisi has cogently rebutted. Daryâbandari,
whom an Iranian friend of his in Austin was eager to have
Texas invite for a lecture last year (I looked over his ré-
sumé and didn't see anything much on Persian literature
in it), voiced a Tudeh-Party line in his interview, calling
Hedâyat deranged and *The Blind Owl* senseless, and
terming Nima pathetic. His predictable conclusion was
that the best piece of modernist Persian literature was
Afghani's *Âhu Khânom's Husband* (1961). Naturally,
Afghani was Daryabandari's Tudeh-Party confrère.
Someone here told me that Tudeh Party membership stays

with Iranians in memory and affection into old age like
Boy Scout experiences. But Boy Scouts learn useful things,
help society, and grow up.

Meanwhile, there is talk of making Âl-e Ahmad's house
a museum, a process about to get underway in the case of
Nima Yushij's house up the same cul-de-sac.

Daneshvar still willingly shoulders the burden of being
Âl-e Ahmad's widow, a duty she considers part of her intellectual struggle as an *engagé* Iranian. As she herself
says, Jacqueline Kennedy should not have married
Aristotle Onassis. Her dealing with Âl-e Ahmad's death
likewise makes paradoxical sense. She insists that it is
symbolic precisely because it was not murder for the very
symbolic virtue which Shams would find in it as assassination. Her feelings about the significance of her own
work, including her faulty judgement in and about the
afterword to *Daneshvar's Playhouse* (1989), likewise find
a sympathetic ear in me as I view the local scene. Although
less dramatic than Farrokhzad or Shahrnush Parsipur,
she remains undaunted. At one point in our conversation,
she said, "You know, even the best husband is not good."
She says she has read *A Lonely Woman.* She is very conscious of the presence of Tahereh Saffarzadeh, and solici-
tous toward such expatriate women writers as Goli
Taraghi.

Tehran, Sunday, December 17th. Yesterday, the 25th of
Âzar, was Mother's Day here, unofficially of course, because the date, I'm told, commemorates the motherhood of
the Shah's third and most fertile wife, Farah Pahlavi.
Otherwise, how long ago and irrelevant the Pahlavi royal
family seems here after a decade without them and their
monarchy. Appropriately enough, I spent the day with two
mother figures: a long walk and lunch with Gertrude Nye
Dorry and hours of conversation and dinner with Simin
Daneshvar. Coincidentally, the two of them collaborated
on a project years ago, the text and translation of the Iran
National Carpet Company's bilingual volumes called
Masterpiece [sic] *of Persian Carpet* (1973) and *Persian
Carpet Appreciation* (1974). They offer conflicting accounts about who wrote and who translated. They share
another coincidental situation, devotion to adopted
daughters. Almost everything Simin had to say about

Jalal contradicts what Shams said, except about his father's predictably pivotal and dominant role.

One day Simin and Jalal were visiting his mother. She was adjusting a grandchild's *nanu* hammock, when Mr. Âl-e Ahmad walked in with a package of apples which he put on a shelf. Jalal's mother got up thinking the apples were for her. Her husband roared that they were for his other wife (who had gotten acquainted with him by asking him as the neighborhood religious elder to take her on his *hajj* caravan to Mecca) and reached out and pushed aside the *nanu*. It swung back and hit Jalal's mother in the chest. She doubled over in pain. Mr. Âl-e Ahmad said nothing. Simin told Jalal to get up to leave.

Years earlier, after Jalal had left home and while he was living in a room at Nader Naderpour's house, he came back to his father's house one day and was in his old room which was now Shams's. They were listening to a record player. Their father walked in, cursed them, and knocked the record player over with his cane.

By the middle of my evening with Dr. Daneshvar, I was feeling admiration for her commitment to a *darvish* life. Her living room, opening on to a courtyard, has a Tabriz *boteh* design carpet on the floor, a kerosene space heater in one corner, a picture of her father over her bed in another corner, a table with two chairs, a Gauguin-like scene painted by a recently deceased brother on the wall above the door, a small bedside table, and a bookcase filled with books. She had just received a handful of books by Mohsen Makhmalbaf which Ms. Roksafat, editor of *Kayhân-e farhangi*, had brought that morning. The room is spare and functional, the life in it lived simply and in the service of thinking and art. Not long ago, her daughter Lili Riyahi had brought her a color Sony television from Dubai, the only piece of up-to-date technology in the room. Cigarettes must burn up half of her university retirement income.

In mid-afternoon today, I took a taxi again to Tajrish and whiled away three hours with books, tea, and conversation at Zamineh Bookstore. Then it was dinner at the Emamis. The new McGill University catalogue had arrived for Hasti who is thinking about studying architecture there, where her older sister goes to school. Karim is not keen on American university education because of drugs and crime which he thinks are inevitable parts of the scene. At the bookstore I met John Gurney who is in the middle of a biography of Edward Browne. He spoke highly of Wilferd Madelung. At Oxford for twenty years, John has the respect of some Iranian literary people, but has published very little.

Goli, Karim, and I sat in their kitchen for dinner and afterwards retired to a living area with Iranian textiles on furniture around a Kermân cloth-covered table, on it nuts and cookies in bowls. A Qâjâr painting hangs over the sofa on which I was sitting. Salman Rushdie, Anne Tyler, Goli Taraghi, Najaf Daryabandari, and Taghi Modarressi were topics of conversation. Modarressi is attracting attention here these days for the Persian version of his *Book of Absent People* (1988), in part because people know how his wife is. The modernist literary crowd loved his *Yakoliyâ va tanhâ'i-ye u* [Yakoliya and Her Loneliness] (1954?) years ago. I preferred *Sharijjân Sharijjân* (1965), which critics mostly ignored. As for the English version of *Absent People*, it's an okay read, but not as engaging for me as Nahid Rachlin's *Foreigner* (1983) and *Married to a Stranger* (1978).

The most intriguing Iranian-authored fiction in English, however, has to be Manuchehr Parvin's *Cry for My Revolution, Iran* (1987). In it, Parvin daydreams aloud a strident, black-and-white oppositionist vision and version of twentieth-century history, all in an idiosyncratic prose much beholden to Persian. My review of it, written at the request of the *International Journal of Middle East Studies*, he considers part of the conspiracy with which America has oppressed Iran since World War II. Regardless, Parvin deserves respect for frankly voicing thoughts which many like-minded Iranians hesitate to admit having.

In the middle of dinner, Hushang Golshiri called. Goli took a message, that I call him to discuss an article in *Sociology of the Iranian Writer*. Moh Ghanoonparvar wrote the piece. So whatever the problem, the two friends from Esfahân can take care of it without me in the middle. Why do many Iranians react with smiles to Esfahan accents? Mr. Naderpour asserts in dead seriousness that people with Esfahan accents should refrain from reciting Persian poetry in public.

Karim also showed me a second living room which faces south and has a window from floor to ceiling. He had the glass in it replaced after an Iraqi missile which exploded down the street caused the previous window to shatter, driving several arrowhead shapes of glass into the wall and ripping a hole in a large Sepehri painting on the opposite wall. He and Goli have left the pieces of glass in the wall and the hole in the painting.

Tehran, Monday, December 18th. While browsing in Payvand Bookstore this morning, from behind me came a voice calling out "âqâ-ye hilman . . . shomâ'in?" [Mr. Hillmann. . . is that you?]. It was the brother of the owner of Payâm Bookstore. All smiles, he quickly ushered me next door to Payam. Time stopped. The three of us rewound it in talk of Sa'edi (it was a hangout of his), Baraheni's literary quarrels, Samad Behrangi's death at twenty-eight and popularity, and the weekly literary gossip of those days, much of it mirrored in *Ferdowsi*, which we all hurried to buy and read each Monday. After a further hour or two at other bookstores, still warm from a sense of belonging, I walked to Villa Street for lunch at Paprika, now called Nâder. A thirtyish man from Turkey sat next to me. Although a resident of Tehran for two years, he doesn't speak Persian. As for his English, he ordered "compost" instead of "compote" for dessert.

In the afternoon, I paid Shams Âl-e Ahmad another visit. On the way, I walked from Kennedy Square down Nosrat-e Gharbi Street to see our first Tehran apartment, where we lived during my '69-'70 Fulbright year. I found the building, saw our second floor porch and windows, recalled pleasant evenings on the porch with Maman and Sorayya, and wondered what had happened to the landlord's servant Barat'ali. He and I took a bus one day to the Shâh'abol'azim Shrine. It momentarily saddened me that I actually did not recognize anything about the building or Nosrat-e Gharbi Street

Shams's son ushered me into his father's library where Shams was reading while resting on his makeshift bed there. He talked as if we had known each other for years. I like him. He described how he found employment in 1963 at Bonyâd-e Farhang-e Irân, which P.N. Khânlari had established. Dr. Daneshvar intimated that Jalal wasn't happy that Shams was working for Khânlarî. But Shams says he found the job because of Jalal and with the latter's encouragement.

I walked back to the apartment feeling good about the biography project. However, once there I realized I had left my notebook with eight days of notes in it at Shams's house. I'll go retrieve it tomorrow morning. In the back of my mind, for no reason, a scenario of the notebook finding its way into the hands of the authorities and a session of questions and answers with them has me a trifle anxious.

With no other plans for tomorrow, I'll do some aimless talking to literary people, browse in bookstores, and walk past memories in neighborhoods where we used to live. Eliza probably cannot recall many images from Tehran. She was only three when we left. But, and it sometimes seems strange, she and Tehran will always have a relationship merely because she was born here. Our obstetrician was playing golf when we called from Karaj to say that Sorayya was on her way. Jim Ricciardi drove us in his Volkswagen Beetle to Alborz Hospital.

Eliza learned to walk at Kucheh-ye Giv, and spoke Persian, her first language, with a Tehran accent. One of her very first words, however, beyond *bâbâ* and *mâmân* and *poof* [food], was *qorbâbâ* [Turkish for "frog"; Persian is *qorbâqeh*], which she uttered when she saw one in front of our house in Rezâ'iyeh, now again called Orumiyeh, one day in the summer of '72.

She was the only child on Kucheh-ye Giv with two Christmas trees, two tricycles (Farzaneh Taymurian got her one the same year Sorayya and I did), and, at one point, two maid-companions, Soghra and Fati. Who knows, she may visit Tehran again one day and take pleasure in retracing her first steps.

How would today's Tehran strike her, or Mike and Judie Jerald's Mitra, or John Newton's Katie, or John and Golriz Lorentz's Davina, American young women with an Iranian heritage? They might not feel that different or disadvantaged as women at social gatherings or in bookstores or in uptown restaurants where they might receive brotherly treatment. But to earn that respect out of the house, they would be covered from head to foot and pass by signs demanding Islamic veiling by women expect-

ing goods and services. On the street, they wouldn't stare at
people or things, but rather look forward or down and
communicate that they were on their way somewhere important.

As I write, Yashar is performing heart-warming service
as my shadow. His American *showhar-'ammeh* can do
nothing wrong. He now knows who Hâfez, Farrokhzad and
Âl-e Ahmad were. I haven't the heart to tell him about
Karim's article on Zabihollah Mansuri in *Nashr-i Dânish*
because Yashar thinks the world of books which Mansuri
has translated.

Tehran, Tuesday, December 19th. Nothing I hear or see
these days contradicts my guesses in *Iranian Culture: A
Persianist View*. University Press of America may be only
a copy-editor-less step up from vanity presses, but I
remain comfortable with my conjectures and conclusions.
I had thought it would be a book easy to place. But starting
with University of Texas Press, everyone turned it down as
unlikely to sell. However, here in the middle of things, the
farthest thing from my mind and the least possible enterprise is characterization of this scene. Life here is much
too variegated, nuanced, layered, and just plain complicated for characterization.

Still, all day today, one thought kept coming to mind,
which everything I see seems to verify: whatever the positive aims the actors in and supporters of the Revolution
had in mind in 1978 and 1979, they cannot suppose the
Revolution has yet succeeded. The Revolution did accom-
plish three important things within its first year. First, it
removed monarchy from the Iranian present and future.
Second, it developed possibly permanent political awareness on the part of many previously apolitical Iranians.
Third, it slowed down wholesale and unthinking adoption
of Western ways. Beyond these three achievements, however, I do not hear much positive commentary by Iranian
acquaintances about the first decade of Islamic Republic
rule.

The expatriate adult Iranians who wanted an end to the
Pahlavi regime and who watched with anticipation from
abroad as events unfolded have no lingering hopes for the
Revolution and live in Iran or visit it only if they have to
for money or family reasons.

The Iranian students abroad who drove from everywhere in Europe to the outskirts of Paris to pay their respects to Ruhollah Khomeini in 1978 have no hopes left for the Revolution either, regardless of their political views.

In Iran, excepting Shi'ite clerics, the various groups of Iranians who demonstrated and suffered and persevered and then welcomed Khomeini back now have confused and sad looks on their faces. They haven't even gotten the satisfaction of revelations in law courts of Pahlavi oppression, corruption, and incompetence. The Islamic Republic has chosen not to reveal documentation of Pahlavi errors and sins.

As for the clergy, they have tainted their Revolution for all time, not through the execution of Pahlavi military and other officials, but through their pogrom against Baha'i Iranians. Secular-minded intellectuals doubt that good can ever come of a Shi'i revolutionary order with Baha'i blood on its hands? And now, the Iran-Iraq war over and life-and-death issues in daily life needing the management decisions, the clergy demand that husbands and wives participate in single-sex aerobic exercise groups in public parks and argue whether the war dead should be buried in their own clothes or in shrouds. The clergy can't decide if the war dead are martyrs, the only people buried in their own clothes. The religious authorities are even planning a grand official welcome for Romanian President Nicolae Ceausescu next week.

This year, more than 600,000 high school graduates will vie for 50,000 college freshman places next fall. Nearly half of those 50,000 places will go to war veterans and relatives of war dead. The remaining and unlucky 550,000 students with diplomas in hand will have three options: take the entrance examination again next year; give up the idea of a college education; or try to go to school abroad, which is prohibitively expensive, particularly in the States, because of devalued Iranian currency.

Tehran, Wednesday, December 20th. She was dressed smartly in black and in accordance with Islamic regulations, but without a trace of the Islamic Republic in what she wore and how she wore it. She had unpainted, manicured fingernails. Her eyes, a touch of Central Asia around

them and set in an expressive face, promised that they
would take in everything.

Early in the conversation–at Ali Dehbashi's library,
which she had rushed into as if late for some internal
deadline or as if behind some spiritual schedule–
Shahrnush Parsipur matter-of-factly announced her age.
She told us that the third edition of *Tubâ va ma'nâ-ye shab*
[Tuba and the Meaning of Night] would appear in 15,000
copies the following week. She chain-smoked, occasionally asking if the smoke bothered us. She continued talking. "My ex-husband and I get along. So do I with another
man I almost married after my divorce. So I haven't re-
married. Of course, I spent four years and seven months in
prison. One night I heard more than two hundred gun
shots. I was the oldest person in every prison section they
put me. They never charged me with a crime. I am not
afraid any more. Gholamhosayn Sa'edi was afraid, of his
mother to begin with. Maybe that accounts for why he
married late. "

"My new novel is about a female Don Quixote. It is
called *'Aql-e âbirang* [Blue-colored Reason]. I write all
night. Last night I didn't sleep. People can say what they
want. They suspected me because of my American fiancé,
as if that made me a member of some three-letter organization. The new novel is more than a thousand pages long.
Baraheni can't forgive people who come into the world
with something. The other night when I saw him at
Morgh-e Âmin Bookstore, he stood on the top step in front
of the shop to tower over me. That's the way things are."

"I started writing the new book after getting out of jail.
People accuse me of expropriating Daneshvar's turf, just
because she is a woman and so am I. This smoke doesn't
bother you, does it? My interview with Nahid Musavi
should be out any day now. It is mostly about *Tuba*. Before
the Revolution everyone confused me with insinuations
about my living in the States. How does publishing translations work in the States?"

Parsipur talked with an ancient mariner's insistence. I
wondered what her crime was. She talked twice as fast and
twice as much as one might expect, perhaps expecting to
get only half a hearing, a female literary parallel to
Islamic inheritance and testimony laws. She knows that
she matters as a writer, but that doesn't make being the

Iranian she is any less difficult. In our conversation, she didn't seem aware of the cultural significance and political implications of her latest book, a short novel called *Zanân bedun-e mardân* [Women without Men]. She didn't even mention it.

Women without Men tells the story of five manifestations of Iranian woman. Early on, I sense that these women are participating in time and place differently from how I do as a male. But that is not inherently troublesome because willing readers of fiction are supposed to accept unfamiliar representations of participation in time and place as part of old-fashioned suspension of disbelief.

Readers first meet a former teacher called Mahdokht Parhami who is spending the summer with her older brother and his family at their garden in Karaj. Life has confused and sometimes terrifies Mahdokht. She can't stand conflict. It upsets her to see colors reflected in the garden stream in apparent conflict. She can't deal with sexuality. She forsook teaching immediately after a male colleague invited her to the movies one day several years ago. Just recently, she came upon her brother's young gardener and a servant girl having sexual intercourse in the shack at the far end of the garden property. She momentarily wanted people to find out about the incident, which would have led to the girl's death at the hands of her male relatives. Mahdokht also has a world of her own thoughts. One is that she could have hundreds of hands with which to knit mittens for children. Another is that the plant world is better than the human. Another is that her *bekârat* [virginity] is like a tree." Another thought, one she acts upon, is a desire to become a tree. At summer's end, she remains in the garden and plants herself. Family shame at her action leads her brother to put the garden up for sale, below market value. No one will likely buy a garden with a tree-woman on the property.

The second of the five "women without men" is a twenty-eight-year-old maiden lady called Fa'ezeh. She has long had her calculating, yet virginal eye on her friend's brother Amir Khân. In fact, in the midst of all of the civil unrest in August 1953, when Prime Minister Mohammad Mosaddeq first forced the Shah to flee Iran and then was himself ousted a week later in an American-supported

coup d'état, Fa'ezeh blithely rides across Tehran to pay her
friend Munes a visit with the ulterior motive of seeing
Amir Khân. Later, when Amir Khân decides to marry, he
surprises his mother by deciding not on Fa'ezeh but on a
teenaged girl, citing the proverb which says that "one can
only weep for a woman over twenty." As it turns out, his
young bride is not a virgin, a devastating piece of news
Amir Khân has to live with.

But before that marriage takes place, readers also meet
Munes, Amir Khân's thirty-eight year old sister and
Fa'ezeh's best friend. One day Fa'ezeh happens to tell
Munes that what the latter has always thought of as
pardeh-ye bekârat [curtain/veil of virginity = hymen] she
has learned from a book is really just a *surâkh* [hole]. This
piece of information disorients Munes who has devoted
her life to protecting her *pardeh*. For example, she has
never climbed a tree. Several days later, Munes throws
herself off the top of her house and dies.

Miraculously, she comes to life again and wanders
about Tehran on her own. She even gets up the nerve to buy
a book called *The Secret to Sexual Satisfaction.* When she
finally returns home, her brother Amir Khân, enraged at
the ruination of the family reputation which Munes's inexplicable and inexcusable absence has caused, kills her.
As for Fa'ezeh, hoping still to catch her man, she helps the
now distraught murderer bury his sister out back. But
when a family servant later visits Fa'ezeh with the news of
Amir Khân's imminent marriage, a now vengeful Fa'ezeh
enlists the servant's assistance in revealing the murder.
While exuming the evidence, they discover that Munes is
very much alive and very hungry. She has also changed.
She can now read people's thoughts and has a different
view of life. She wants to experience everything, through
travel.

Parsipur now introduces readers to another woman
who is still very much with a man, her sneering, abusive
husband of thirty-two years ("Darling, next month you'll
be fifty-one . . . by the way, when a woman reaches
menopause, do her feelings change?"). The wife, Farrokh
Leqa, detests him in turn and often thinks about a man
whom she loved years ago and who, when they first met
under an acacia tree, said she looked like Vivien Leigh's
younger sister. That lover married an American and died

in the States in an automobile accident. Farrokh Leqa en-
joys being alone with her daydreams. She wishes she had
a garden in Karaj. On one particularly tense evening at
home, Farrokh Leqa's husband uncharacteristically feels
affection toward his wife. He addresses her with tender-
ness, but barely gets his mouth open when the shock of his
unprecedented, unanticipated demeanor causes Farrokh
Leqa to push him away. He loses his balance and falls
down the stairs to his death. Farrokh Leqa buys the
Parhami garden in Karaj.

Meanwhile a prostitute called Zarrin Kolah, who is
with thirty or more men every day, decides to leave her life
in Tehran's red light district. For six months now every
man she sees is headless. She repents her sinful ways and
makes a pilgrimage to the Shi'ite shrine at Shâh
'Abdol'azim just south of Tehran. She cries her eyes out,
leaving no trace of femininity in her face. She asks where
a person can get a cool drink of water. "Karaj" is the answer. She sets out for Karaj. On the way she meets a man
without a name. He calls himself "Kind Gardener." Because
he is the first man she has seen for months who is not
headless, she insists on staying with him.

By this time, Farrokh Leqa is inspecting the Parhami
garden in Karaj. The price is right, and she doesn't mind
the tree-woman on the property next to the stream. In fact,
she thinks that only she understands the tree. In addition,
she thinks the tree-woman might help her attract a following. Then she might run for Parliament. While she is
making up her mind about the garden, one by one the
other women show up.

Zarrin Kolah and "Kind Gardener" arrive. Farrokh
Leqa hires him immediately. So he and Zarrin Kolah take
up residence in the shack at the far end of the garden.
Zarrin Kolah gets pregnant and becomes translucent, like
glass crystal.

Munes and Fa'ezeh then appear at the garden. A
drunken truck driver and his assistant had raped them on
their way to Karaj, the first leg of what they thought would
be a trip around the world. Immediately afterwards, both
men died in a freak accident as their truck struck two trees
by the side of the highway. Fa'ezeh has been crying hyster-
ically ever since. Munes says, "Okay, so I had virginity
once and don't have it any longer. It's no big loss." Fa'ezeh

moans, "Yes, but you're thirty-eight, and I, who am only twenty-eight, still had hopes of marriage."

Zarrin Kolah gives birth to a lily. With her milk, Kind Gardener feeds the Tree-Woman. As a tree, Mahdokht grows branches and leaves and one year produces seeds. In fact, her treeness comprises those seeds, and she finally bursts into seeds which wind and river will take to all corners of the earth.

Farrokh Leqa decides to sell the garden. She returns to Tehran in the company of a young artist who was painting portraits of her. The artist's first exhibition is a failure. So Farrokh Leqa packs him off to Europe for further study. She then marries an old friend who knew her lover years ago. She and her new husband live an okay life. Her husband becomes a member of Parliament, while she becomes the honorary director of an orphanage. He gets sent on an important government mission to Europe, while she gets to go with him.

Fa'ezeh becomes the second wife of Amir Khân, who gets another job to pay for the second-floor apartment he has to provide for her because she won't live under the same roof with his first wife. Fa'ezeh's life is so-so, neither good nor bad.

Munes had helped Kind Gardener feed Mahdokht. As she gets ready to leave the garden, Kind Gardener reminds her of what has happened to Mahdokht, who will have to start all over again through seeds, and admonishes Munes to seek out the darkness which light will follow, to "go and become a human being." Munes pirhouettes like a whirling dervish, rises into the sky and is transported by a black cloud which deposits her in an endless desert. For seven years she traverses seven deserts. Full of experience, she returns to Tehran, washes, puts on clean clothes, and becomes a teacher.

At the very end of the book, as Kind Gardener and Zarrin Kolah are themselves preparing to leave the garden, he tells her they will not need their clothes or other belongings on their trip. She acquiesces. They then sit atop the lily to which she had given birth. It envelopes them. They turn into smoke and ascend into the sky.

Women without Men makes Parsipur heir to Forugh Farrokhzad. In her story Parsipur does not take the sort of autobiographical risks which Farrokhzad took in her lyric poetry because her focus is not on herself as a character. Parsipur's focus in on "woman," for her, "Iranian woman." She has moved from Farrokhzad's focus on self to a focus on the womanhood which may be the largest part of self. Nevertheless, in choosing the particular images for her depiction of woman and in representing her woman-centeredness, she takes artistic and cultural risks as bold as Farrokhzad's earlier autobiographical risks.

One of those risks is trying to make non-Iranian narrative techniques Iranian. No major work of Persian fiction exhibits more Western influence than Hedayat's *The Blind Owl*. Yet no Persian prose work has more mesmerized Iranian readers and struck more inexplicable chords in their Iranian hearts. In short, Hedayat's aesthetic eclecticism in his *chef-d'oeuvre* signals a hallmark of Persian art at least since the beginning of the construction of Persepolis in 520 B.C.E. This makes meaningless the inevitable establishment charge of *gharbzadegi* [weststruckness] or lack of Iranian authenticity in future criticisms of Parsipur's book because it embodies techniques perhaps inspired by *One Hundred Years of Solitude*. Because of her straightforward and palpably Iranian *yeki bud yeki nabud* [once-upon-a-time] narrative mode, her deft touches of Iranian illuminationist and other gnostic images, and her Iranian skill at weaving variegated warps and wefts into an Iranian design, Parsipur makes readers feel at home in her tale regardless of where some of its techniques may have came from.

In addition, Parsipur trusts her Iranian woman's imagination not to let her down when it leads her fiction into realms which defy laws which Iranian men have catalogued for physical nature. Having suspended their disbelief at the outset of her fiction, male readers are carried along in incidents which defy male clinical observation. The men in the novel mostly behave in realistic ways and in accordance with laws of everyday physics. It is the women who defy those laws, who come back from the dead, who see men without heads, who become trees, who can read people's minds, and who give birth to lilies. If Garcia Marquez uses preternatural happenstances to give an air of universal timelessness to his fiction, Parsipur employs similar techniques to force readers to accept the possibility that a woman-centered universe differs from a

male-centered universe and to persuade readers that
woman's internal world has realities, including images,
different from and beyond those which males have determined, defined, and approved.

At the same time, Parsipur's perspective in *Women
without Men* does not proceed from a demonstration of the
horrors of the world which men have created for women to
live in to a rejection by women of that world. Parsipur's
women cannot live fulfilling lives without men. In this regard, perhaps Parsipur's real audience is not women readers, but male readers, who, deservedly or not, have the real
power to change things, even the way society thinks and
educates. Those readers can appreciate the unfair and
sometimes absurd world which they have organized and
in which woman can function only as women, not as hu-
mans. Daneshvar's *Savushun* probably implies a similar
view. However, Daneshvar chooses not to admit that
Iranian women cannot do it themselves or that women
raised in an Iranian environment may not have inherited
the resources to carve out a human niche for themselves.
So Daneshvar engages in wishful thinking in having Zari
become heroic at the end of *Savushun.* Parsipur has yet to
create a heroic woman. Of course, there is one in her non-
fictive world, herself, a person who would appear not to
have found happiness and who may not survive the tumult
she has stirred up around herself, but who remains
woman while being human.

(End of session. I should be forgiven lapses into classroom tone and advocacy every so often in these journal
entries.)

Tehran, Thursday, December 21st. Dr. Daneshvar says
that she has not signed a contract with Mage Publishers
for the translation of *Savushun* and that she stipulated
that I write its introduction. I told her that my only con-
nection with the project was suggesting Moh
Ghanoonparvar as a translator to Mage without knowing
anything about their disposition of Roxanne Zand's version. Mage's publication of *Savushun* will bring to nearly
a dozen the number of Iranian novels available in
English: Hedayat's *The Blind Owl* (1941), Alavi's *Her Eyes*
(1952), Âl-e Ahmad's *The School Principal* (1958) and *By
the Pen* (1962), Chubak's *Tangsir* (1963) and *The Patient*

Stone (1966), Golshiri's *Prince Ehtejâb* (1969), Baraheni's *The Infernal Days of Mr. Ayâz* (1972), and Fasih's *Sorayyâ in a Coma* (1983). Except for *Her Eyes, The School Principal*, and *Ayâz*, they are all successful fictions.

In the list, *Savushun* has a special place. By all reports, it is the best-selling Iranian novel ever. Farzaneh Milani asserts that 400,000 copies have been sold, which would mean that twenty percent of the adult Persian-speaking population has bought the book. (100,000+ seems a more realistic figure; ditto for the Iranian population in the greater Los Angeles area).

Farzaneh, Moh, and others call *Savushun* a masterpiece. It has incontrovertible significance as the first major Iranian novel by a woman author and as a novel with a female protagonist. But the prose has only a single register, regardless of who is talking or what is happening. More importantly, the change in Zari's character after Yusof's death seems implausible, and not behavior which makes sense on the basis of her earlier thoughts and deeds. My guess is that Âl-e Ahmad's own popularity abetted sales of his widow's book. The anti-establishment and anti-English story, even if set in the early 1940s, likewise has obvious appeal to many Iranian readers.

At the same time, Zari's character is a telling and presumably fairer depiction of a woman than those females who people fictions by Âl-e Ahmad, Chubak, Golshiri, and Sa'edi. Her self-doubts, wonderment at her lot as a woman, and confusion at male warring persuade me to recognize that Zari sees the world as she does not just because she is an individual, but because she as a woman perceives differently from how I can.

The Mage people think that Roxanne Zand's translation suffers from unidiomatic or substandard English in many places. Very few translations from native Persian to foreign English don't, Taghi Modarressi's notion of "writing with an accent" aside. Somewhere down the Persianist road, if ever imaginative Persian literature is to find an audience in English garb, it will need translators with skills other than fluency in English and Persian. They need to be writers in English.

The commitment of Iranians in the English-speaking world to introducing their national literature to a new audience through the thankless enterprise of translation is commendable. But few published translations of Persian poems, plays, short stories, and novels could survive critiques in a creative writing class. Moreover, the translations appear under such imprints as Persian Heritage, Mazdâ, and Mage, which cater mostly to Iranians and other readers who may know Persian. That is no criticism of such publishers. But it does highlight another another issue. Mage, for example, thinks of itself as offering an authentic, self-view of Persian Iranian literature for those Iranians whose intellectual language has become English. I wonder how Iranian intellectuals can be once they no longer think in Persian.

Tehran, Friday, December 22nd. Maliheh, Yashar, Sara and I were guests for lunch today at the Mazaheris'. Our telephone taxi snaked westwardly through neighborhoods which did not exist fifteen years ago. The Mazaheris' neighborhood looked deceptively settled and mature, as if it had been there for fifty years, shades of Khosrow Shahani's *Vahshatâbâd* [Terrorville] (1967). Our driver took a serpentine route to avoid traffic and roadblocks set up for the Friday community prayers at what used to be the soccer field at Tehran University.

Aqdas Khânom, who looks the same as she did twenty years ago, prepared an attractive meal, with much more to eat than we guests could devour over several days, and with ice cream for dessert. Iranian cookbooks should deal more with this culture of Iranian eating. Multiple main dishes invariably get served so that guests will be sure to find something they like. Much more than enough appears on the table so that guests need not think about how much they should eat. Dinners with guests seem an earthly moment rivalling dreams of heavenly variety and abundance. Mother, who has always prepared the one main course she has decided the guests will like and who has always prided herself on having no leftovers even with guests, would be horrified at dinner parties here or even at our home in Austin.

Hormoz and his wife were there with their two children. I talked politics with Hormoz and Mr. Mazaheri for two hours. Hormoz has an anti-American edge to his determination to see life in Iran as good. When it was time for him to continue his education abroad as his brothers did, he chose to stay in Tehran. Mr. Mazaheri reminisced about his years in prison during the aftermath of the Mosaddeq coup d'état. I won't find time to visit any other relatives this coming week. But dinner at the Mehravaris several nights ago and today's lunch satisfy the most important familial duties. I had good times in both places and showed our family pictures to all present. As for the Mokasebis, a letter explaining why I cannot come to Mashhad will have to suffice. I still haven't met my niece Faraneh and my youngest nephew, Armen.

Shab-e yaldâ [night of the winter solstice], which was last night, found me at the Emamis again. I sipped *mâ'oshsha'ir* all evening, ate a reasonable amount of Shirazi fare, including a sort of pasty *fesenjân* blended with yoghurt, and revelled and wallowed in conversation with the dozen or so other guests. Bizhan Jalali brought a copy of a collection of his poetry for me to give to the Texas library, as well as a previously unpublished picture of Sadeq Hedayat, showing the writer relaxed and happy, cigarette in hand, unaware that his picture was being taken.

I wanted the conversation to turn to poetry, especially with Jalali and Ali Mohammad Haghshenas there. The latter wrote an intriguing review of a collection of Simin Behbahani's *ghazals* in *Naqd-e âgâh* six or seven years back. In it he argues that Behbahani employs unfamiliar metrical schemes as a technique of *âshnâ'î-zadâ'i* [defamiliarization] to predispose readers for her non-traditional *ghazal* content and tone. This, Haghshenas opines, constitutes a "Nima'ic" thrust in the realm of *ghazal*, just as Nima Yushij had changed Persian poetry in general from a perfective to an evolutionary mode by disturbing metrical feet as defamiliarization prefatory to offering brand-new poetic content. What Haghshenas leaves unsaid, but implied, is that Behbahani is showing that the past can belong in the present and the future, that traditional Iranian readers need not worry that they have to give up or reject something long cherished in getting comfortable with modernist Persian poetry or that Nima's influence will lead to a poetic dead end or chaos.

The party lasted until after midnight, when Goli called a telephone taxi for John and Faraneh Gurney and myself. On the way to the Gurneys' house on Mir Damad Street, we saw khaki-dressed young men armed with rifles and ma-

chine guns in the middle of the highway. Our taxi driver
called them "Basiji." They didn't stop us. But once we let
the Gurneys off and returned to the highway, the young
men flagged us down, interrogated the driver, ordered me
out of the car, and asked for identification. All I had with
me was my University of Texas faculty identification
card. The young man with the flashlight read it the way
you do when you want to show that you understand something you don't understand. But he could read the picture.
So he nodded approval. I smiled at seeing how useful my
university I.D. was in revolutionary Iran. I can barely get
books out of the library with it at UT and can't even get a
check cashed with it at an Austin supermarket. On hearing that I was an American, another of the armed young
men gave me a lecture on the need for me to tell
"Perezident Boosh" and the American people the truth
when I return home and to warn him against future fool-
ish ventures such as the invasion of Panama. After polite
"good evenings," the young men allowed us to continue on
our way. Strangely enough, nothing about the incident
worried me. It seemed almost natural to me, who once
quickly got off a bus in Chicago's Hyde Park neighborhood
merely because a teenager near the front was toying with a
revolver he had pulled out of his pocket.

The same holds for my brief visit to Hotel-e Jânbâzân-e
Eslâmi on Pahlavi Street, on the way to the Emamis', to
ask someone to call me a taxi. Hotel guests in the lobby,
mostly disabled war veterans, cast me stern looks. But
that didn't bother me. Iranians deserve to give Americans
stern looks. Moreover, the looks were etched on faces as a
result of war experience and not as a reaction to me. When
the desk clerk offered to send an employee to take me to
Tajrish after failing to locate a telephone taxi, that
seemed natural too. The drive took ninety minutes, with a
half-hour wait in a traffic jam at Vanak Square.

With no Friday plans, I took Yashar for a walk and
window-shopping down Fâtemi and Pahlavi Streets this
morning. We meandered though the park and raced up one
of its hills. Then we paid the Museum of Modern Art a
visit.

"Yashar, look at these three paintings, with boulders
and sturdy, straight tree trunks. Sohrab Sepehri painted
them. He usually does not put people in his paintings, or

realistic city life. Perhaps he just loves nature. Or perhaps he thinks he can keep his idealism going only if he paints pieces of nature, not people or things people make."

"Yashar, take a look at these paintings of numbers and colors. Who painted them? Hossein Zenderoudi. Do you know that he did the cover of my Farrokhzad book? No, I don't know him personally. But doesn't he make the numbers look like pieces of a garden, so much grander and more colorful than the world of real numbers and real gardens?"

"Do you see the different browns in this village scene? It's by Parviz Kalantari. O yes, he's famous too. Yashar, which paintings do you like best? These over here? O yes, these are watercolors. Let's see who painted them. They are all by the same painter, Yasa'i Shajanian. No, Yashar, I have never seen his work before. But he makes Esfahan look so peaceful and important. And look at these miniature-style paintings. Here's one of two women weaving a *gelim*."

I walked up and down both sides of Ferdowsi Street on Tuesday. Only about fifteen carpet stores remain. Mike Jerald and I had counted one hundred fifteen stories in a survey we did in the summer of '75. A friend of Habib Nohiyan's said Habib, whom I owe 750 *tomans* from 1973, is now working in New York. I'm happy for him. His partner still runs Churchill's here, now on Ferdowsi itself, in an arcade. The shop where I heard about Habib was dark, with not enough light to make the carpets on the walls even slightly communicate their garden message. Huddled in the corner, an Aladin heater in the middle of them, sat five middle-aged and older Jewish merchants, themselves drab, apprehensive, and not sure what now to make of an American whom they would have greeted with enthusiasm and a glass of tea fifteen years ago in hopes that a carpet of theirs might end up under his arm on the way out of their shop. Images of small groups of men in nameless places in Eastern Europe and Russia came to my mind during the conversation.

Tehran, Saturday, December 23rd. During our years in Tehran, Sorayya and I never visited royal palaces, government museums, or other tourist attractions. Today, when tourists no longer visit Tehran, I found myself on the grounds and in the rooms of Sa'dâbâd Palace with Parviz and Pari Ahour. We looked at the monumental Kerman and Mashhad carpets on its cold marble and parquet floors and wondered at the collections of European furniture and bric-à-brac. We walked more quickly than we might have because we had to leave our shoes at the front door.

We walked at the foot of the Alborz Mountains in Darband and then lunched on barley soup and Bakhtiyârî kabob at the Hotel Darband on Sa'dâbâd Square. We had thought about eating *âbgusht* at a cliffside stand, in bowls full of bubbling, orangish broth set on red hot coals. But we guessed that the food might haunt us later. On the deck of the café, I took a snapshot of Pari and Parviz which the café owner managed to get himself into.

A letter from Afzal Vossoughi was waiting for me back at Maliheh's apartment. He says he plans to buy a ticket to come to Tehran on Thursday to see me. No tickets are available in Tehran for Mashhad until late March, after New Year's. I've written him an express letter saying that I'll leave my Thursday and Friday open should he actually come, but that he mustn't feel compelled to visit because our not seeing one another would be my fault in any case. You take express letters here to a neighborhood office and pay a nominal amount for a service called *tipâks*. They put the letter on the next plane to its domestic destination. It gets delivered in the next day's mail. If I remember correctly, the Achaemenid postal service twenty-five hundred years ago was the world's first.

Before meeting the Ahours this morning, I visited Lili Golestan's art gallery in Darrus. She has her father's sparkle in her face and eyes and speaks in his confident way, with a tinge of softness or friendliness added. On exhibition were landscape photographs by the film director Abbas Kiyarostami. He has an optimistic photographic vision of the inimical countryside, a contemporary man with a not-atypical, traditional artistic eye. He wants to see the world as better than it is, or at least represents it in art as better than it is so that viewers do not get reminders of life's harshness in their flights of fancy in art.

Darrus remains beautiful. After leaving the gallery, I stood across the street and stared at the tall evergreens in the Golestan courtyard, the while thinking about

Farrokhzad and other people whose voices filled that courtyard at times during the 1960s. I couldn't guess the location of Mr. Chubak's house in relation to Mr. Golestan's. People still talk about both of them, although Chubak's achievements in *Tangsir* and *The Patient Stone* are still inadequately appreciated. As for Golestan, people say he plans to sue me over *A Lonely Woman*, as soon as his lawyer finishes suing someone over something about his Eaton Place flat. His case will have to be asserted property rights to a free-spirited woman after her death. My defense will be a spirited recitation of Farrokhzad's own autobiographical poetry.

Goli has twice asked me to comment upon Karim's translations in Shahrokh Golestan's *The Wine of Nishapur* (1988). Golestan's photographs have no Iranian or Khayyamic images in them, perhaps implying his sense of the universality of the Khayyamic mood. But he has the mood wrong–Dashti's vision of Khayyam is closer to historical fact. Golestan's photos are more romantic than Kiyarostami's. The calligraphy in the book also seems overly decorative for Khayyam's serious succinctness. Even Karim's skills are not used to good advantage in the project. Karim can do good things with descriptive and personal lyric poems that do not depend upon concomitant succinctness and tight verse structure for effects. For example, his versions of Farrokhzad and Sepehri read well. But only professional versifiers of English should dare take on Khayyamic quatrains. Even Robert Graves was not up to it in *The Rubaiyyat of Omar Khayyam: A New Translation* (1968), a bizarre volume based on a forged or fake manuscript which a brother of self-styled Sufi guru Idris Shah duped Graves into translating.

One of Karim's versions reads: "Do you remember the palace that ranked high with heaven / and at whose portal kings pressed their cheeks? / Now a dove perches on the top of its battlements / saying: coo coo where oh where?" The translation doesn't have the compactness or rhythm that even the following quickly penned rendition with an ear to iambs and end rhyme exhibits: "In splendor monarchs faced the world / from palace towers which touched the sky. / A dove now perches there instead / and coos and coos: O where and why?" Moreover, the image in the second verse of Karim's version resists imagining.

Tehran, Sunday, December 24th. Upon hearing that my
wife is Iranian, people often nod in understanding. Yes,
the marriage promises free Persian lessons for life. Some
have also long assumed that my work must involve spying. Otherwise, why would an American who knows the
one language which counts everywhere learn Persian in
which there is no money?

It is true that without Sorayya I'd shift to world literature or take up English literature again. As it is, Persian
literature is part of the warp and weft of our lives. Sorayya
knows as much about my work as I do. Moreover, my work
is part of Eliza's heritage and past, which she can visit
through my writing. I haven't worked out why I don't
think of German, Scottish, or Irish literature as a special
part of my own heritage, while I think of Persian literature as a defining part of Eliza's. Of course, the Persian
language and Persian literature have long served as a key
to Iranian heritage in general, from the almost miracu-
lous emergence of the language and its literature in the
aftermath of the Arab Moslem invasion fourteen centuries ago. As Mescoub argues hyperbolically, Iranians
then had almost nothing left but their language and a history told in that language, and no arena for culture-specific self-expression except for imaginative literature.

As for the actual people part of Eliza's Iranian heritage,
it is special and fraught with what makes this place Iran.
Her grandfather Mohammad Ora'ee Abbasian, whose family had lived for centuries in Tabriz and Marand, walked
up the hill to the highway outside Marand one day at sixteen years of age, hitched a ride on a tanker truck, and
never looked back. Eliza's grandmother Hajiyeh Nofayli
was born in Doshambeh, later Stalingrad, and now again
Doshambeh. Her family fled southward after Bolshevik
Revolutionaries confiscated their home and property.
They settled in Mashhad and added Persian to their native
languages Russian and Turkish.

On the way back from a trip to Herat, Mohammad gave
Hajiyeh's brother a ride and other help. The brother told
Mohammad that he had an unmarried sister. Mohammad
and Hajiyeh married and raised a family in Mashhad.
They had nine children. The oldest of the seven who sur-
vived childhood is Paridokht, who was a grade school

principal in Mashhad before the Revolution. The second oldest is Yashar and Sara's father Abbas. After over ten years in Chicago, he returned to Tehran in 1980, became a businessman, and married Maliheh. The third is Sorayya. Then comes Mahin, who graduated from Tehran University with a degree in Philosophy and also married a Peace Corps Volunteer. They now live in Los Angeles. Javad was next. A physician with two small children, he died in a head-on collision late one afternoon in August 1987 driving back to Mashhad from hospital duty in Bojnord. The second youngest Abbasian is Fahimeh, who lives in Göttingen with her husband Sarvar and their two children Nima and Âyda. The youngest is Reza who spent months in solitary confinement at the Khorramshahr prison for innocuous anti-Pahlavi activities when a student at the Âbadan Oil Engineering College. After graduation, he washed his hands of Iran and came to The University of Texas for graduate study and is now a mathematics professor at Texas Lutheran College in Seguin.

My marriage to Sorayya, in fact, changed the geography of the Abbasians as much as the Bolsheviks had done. Abbas joined us in Chicago, Mahin met her husband through me. Pari and her family and Reza came to Austin. As for Eliza's eleven first cousins, they live in Mashhad, Tehran, Göttingen, Miami, Austin, and Los Angeles. None of them speaks Âzarbâyjâni Turkish. The two in L.A. don't speak Persian either. Two are native speakers of German. Six don't speak English. None practices Islam. Theirs is a family tree with a millennium of roots in Turkish-speaking Iran, and one generation of uprootedness.

Tehran, Tuesday, December 26th. Christmas has come and gone. Mine was a pleasant day as a guest for a midday dinner at the Ahours. Gertrude and Moh Dorry were the other guests. I brought corsages for the ladies, and a bouquet arrangement of dried flowers for the Ahours.

In the late afternoon, I walked home from Jordan Boulevard, across to Pahlavi, and down to Dr. Fâtemi, some six miles. On the way I reminisced about my two other Christmases away from family, in 1965 and 1966. Their images have perhaps merged. At the American Consulate in Mashhad, an Irish Dominican priest from Tehran called Father Barden celebrated midnight mass

and delivered two sermons, one in English and the other
in French. The French nuns from the leprosarium sang
hymns. John Newton and I afterwards rode our bicycles
around the Emâm Rezâ Shrine, an instinctive and theo-
logically inefficacious circumambulation. We ate
Christmas dinner at the Bâkhtar Hotel: a dozen fried eggs
and specially-ordered bacon, and a tin of Kraft cheese
from Australia.

I'm seated in the tea room of the Iran Carpet Museum,
yet another garden retreat from Tehran. Low tables with
leather-upholstered couches around them, Esfahan wood
block print cloths on the tables, white calligraphic designs on the wall, cool quiet throughout and in the background whispers of the employees who serve the tea and
cakes. From the cavernous main hall with its monumental Kerman carpets and a portrait of Ruhollah Khomeini
on the walls comes compensatory noise: a busload of high
school girls are buying postcards, chattering and laugh-
ing, and otherwise revelling in a field trip away from
school.

That is also my situation, on a field trip away from one
of the largest schools anywhere. The word "Texas" gets a
smile almost everywhere I use it in response to queries as
to where I do what I do. I might as well smile too because I
really don't know what to make of the place either, I mean
The University of Texas. No university could be more
avowedly American and deliberately parochial. Yet you
hear more foreign languages and see more likely foreign
faces on campus than at almost any other university in
North America. UT is full of itself and of its big business
school and engineering and law programs which promote
capitalistic success as much as anything else. Yet it
routinely makes room for the likes of Persian literature, a
field taught at no more than twenty-five universities in
the English-speaking world. Perhaps the most dynamic
and articulate Iranian professor Texas ever had ended up
suing his department for discrimination. Yet I'm told the
first foreign president of student government at Texas was
an Iranian. A College of Liberal Arts dean once withheld
approval of my course on Persian carpets because of his
doubts about its intellectual content, while our Center for
Middle Eastern Studies has supported exhibitions and
research on Persian textiles as strongly as any museum in

the States. Our University Research Institute once awarded me a six-month salary grant to do research on feminism, while among 1,800 tenure-track faculty here probably no more than eighty women have achieved the rank of full professor.

As aggressively Anglo and Texan as UT and West Austin are, we have many evenings which, eyes closed, sound just like these days in Tehran. But my status in that Iranian world of Austin, on and off campus, is ambiguous. Austin Iranians would prefer that an Iranian be "the professor" of Persian, perhaps in part because Persian plays a special part in their identity. When rumors circulated several years ago that Columbia was thinking of me for its Persian studies chair, Iranians from all over the place reacted. From East Berlin, Bozorg Alavi sent a letter to the editor of *Par Monthly* with this statement: "Dear Friends, The news of Michael Hillmann's selection to succeed Professor Yarshater is truly astonishing. . . If this gentleman's erudition consists in the publication of the Forugh book and her relationship with so-and-so, one can only throw one's hands up in despair. That's all I have to say."

In class, some Iranian students test me during the first weeks of courses. The Zoroastrian student may question my definition of Ahuramazda. A student from Shiraz may have difficulty accepting my *explication de texte* of a Hâfezian *ghazal*. An Iranian-American graduate student once confronted me with the argument that if Iranian students in the class disagree with me, I must be wrong.

Some Iranians who used to be somebody or something else back home and because of the Revolution are in Austin, perhaps for good, have reason to be unhappy with me. Reports of my classroom questioning of the literary relevance and critical appeal of Ferdowsi and Sa'di and my criticisms of patriarchal aspects of Iranian literary culture make them suppose they'd be better served by a more respectful fellow Iranian.

Tehran, Wednesday, December 27th. In mid-morning, I treated myself to an American breakfast at Lâleh International, then strolled through the park and browsed at bookstores across from Tehran University. I found myself at Paprika's again for lunch. During it I wrote a letter to Sadeq Chubak.

"Dear Mr. Chubak, *salâm*, from far away. From very far away. I am sitting–the empty chair across from me, I wish you were in it–in Paprika, waiting for chicken kabob. I am drinking a bottle of *mâ'oshsha'ir*. No more Star, Shams, or Tuborg. And would you believe it, the mere substitution of the Arabic for *âb-e jow* magically eliminates the alcoholic content. How are you? You come to mind often in my meandering daily walks. The tired faces of early paperback editions of *The Puppet Show*, *The Chimpanzee Whose Master Died* and the hardback first edition of *Tangsir* stare up at me from sidewalk displays next to the *jub* on the south side of Shah Reza Street across from the University. In every conversation about novels, *The Blind Owl*, *Prince Ehtejâb* and your *Patient Stone* are the only inevitable topics. The traditionalists still give you some credit for those early short stories and still try to pass you off as a disciple of Hedayat. Ali Dehbashi is planning a volume of critical writing on your work. People here refer to Ali as modernist literature's answer to Mr. Afshar.

I miss those days in the early 1970s and you in those days and dinners at your house: Scotch whiskey and steak and baked potatoes. And your front bathroom's urinal, the only one I've ever seen in an Iranian house. And the arguments with Baraheni. Do you remember the evening in the summer of 1975 after dinner at your house when I talked you into stopping at Hosayn Naraghy's house near Sehrâh-e Arâmaneh to say hello? When Hosayn and his relatives saw their heroic writer in Bermuda shorts and bare feet, well, they loved and never forgot it. I couldn't find your house the other day when I stopped by Lili Golestan's gallery which they have built on to the front of their property. She operated a bookstore there for several years.

You would dislike it here now for the very reasons you bring to life in *Tangsir* and *The Patient Stone*. I'm off to a lecture at the Philosophical Society after lunch, then dinner with a group from the lecture. At the end of the week, I'll fly to Germany to see Sorayya's sister. Then Paris, which we never did visit together as we talked about doing in London that spring. Take care, . . ."

The last time I called Mr. Chubak, his wife Qodsi complained that I did not call him enough, not enough for a
friend. Except for Jalal Matini, Iranian friends my age or
older who have spent most of their lives in Iran often take
umbrage when I do not call them first or regularly, even
after I explain that I almost never use the phone when
there is time to write.

I reached the Philosophical Society half an hour early
and sought out the library, where Ali Ashraf Sadeqi found
me. We had a good chat thanks to his ice-breaking witti-
ness. On the way to the lecture room, several people told
me the Director wanted to see me before the talk. In his office sat a handful of older men, talking quietly. I got the
feeling they expected me to know who they were. The director is Mahmud Borujerdi, a self-assured and pleasant man
whom Farhang Raja'i identified in a confidential whisper
beforehand as Âyatollâh Khomeini's son-in-law.

Dr. Borujerdi asked me before the session what I might
need. My answer: a glass of water at the podium and re-
moval of the tape recorder. Just before introducing me, Dr.
Pourjavady called on a man to say a prayer. The latter in-
toned Arabic for ten minutes. I began to feel uncomfortable at this unexpected context for my remarks, but then
remembered having endured Pahlavi rituals and anthems
even in movie theatres years ago. During the talk–and like
the old days I was thinking in Persian almost as if not
American–the thought came to me that my real audience
are Tehran literary people, that I belong in a place which I
might not tolerate for long. Whatever I call it, ambiva-
lence or dilemma, it almost qualifies me for an Iranian
identity card.

After my talk, the audience of thirty or so assorted academics and others initiated a lively discussion which
moderator Pourjavady ended after ninety minutes. Then,
we adjourned to a basement reception area where Dr.
Borujerdi graciously hosted tea and pastries. Before the
lecture and at the reception I had a chance to talk to
Behruz Neirami and Iraj Afshar who surprised me pleasantly by attending. I had asked that Ali Dehbashi and
Gholamhosayn Yusofi also get invitations. Ali's didn't
reach him, and Dr. Yusofi is seriously ill, terminally ill in
fact. Ali spends considerable time with Dr. Yusofi, who is
determined to complete as many research projects as time

will allow. He is a reason for having the phrase
"gentleman and scholar."

The audience had lots of questions. Why does so little
textual work or preparation of critical texts of Persian
works take place in the States? Why do Iranian
Persianists devote so much time there to translation from
Persian to English? Do Baha'is control Persian studies in
the States? Why does classical literature receive short
shrift there in comparison with contemporary literature?
Why doesn't American Persianism produce work as good
as in Europe? Why don't any Iranian Persian professors in
the States have graduate degrees from Tehran University?

My talk and comments constituted an apology for
American Persian studies, meant at the moment but
sounding hollow afterwards. Although Persian studies in
America has challenged antiquarianism and has offered
discipline orientations to balance or complement orientalist and philological traditions, it is very uneven and
theoretically not up to date. Julie Scott Meisami's
Medieval Persian Court Poetry (1987) and Michael Beard's
forthcoming *Hedayat's Blind Owl as a Western Novel*
(1990?) are the only first-rate American monographs on
Persian literature. Yet even these stimulating comparatist
studies say more about the European side of the ledger
than the Iranian. Among Meisami's more than 280 footnotes, no more than seven or eight are Iranian. Even
Iranian Persianists in the States often ignore scholarship
and research in Iran.

Then a straightforward project such as the University of
Washington Press edition and translation of Ferdowsi's
Rostam and Sohrab (1988) exhibits flaws even at the level
of basic translation. Taken to task for them in my review
in *Iranshenasi*, the translator, in a reply which I had
asked *Iranshenasi* editor Jalal Matini to invite him to
make, merely engages in name-calling, implying that the
scores of instances of errors in construing the Persian and
in scholarship are jaundiced quibbles over matters of
taste and interpretation.

About thirty Persianists, mostly Iranian-born along
with a handful of North American-born and four or five
Europeans, staff the Persian positions at North American
universities. On balance, the scales tip markedly on the
plus side for these teacher-scholars, serious people who

have made good choices in life, including their commendable humanistic dedication to teaching, writing and otherwise promoting Iranian literary culture. American Persianists cannot be faulted for such careers when they pay their own way and dues, and do much more, and do it all much better than it was done in the 1950s and earlier.

The most promising Persianists in the States are the younger Iranian-born scholars, even when they come to the field with undergraduate degrees in mathematics, business, English, or French. The best are those trained in Comparative Literature, and a heterogenous group who deal with Persian literature from non-literary vantagepoints. The best among the latter are Mahmoud Omidsalar, Simin Karimi, Hamid Naficy, and Hamid Dabashi. Although extrinsic in their approaches to imaginative literature, they have solid disciplinary foci and enrich the study of Persian literature with data and insights from psychology, folklore, linguistics, cinema, and sociology.

Now, "extrinsic" does not mean something less than "intrinsic." But Persianist practitioners of extrinsic approaches may need reminding that their work engages imaginative literature other than *qua* imaginative literature. Scholars with extrinsic approaches need to make an explicit case if and when they expect their analyses to account for the literary and aesthetic appeal of the works they study.

Some Iranian-born Persianists in the States treat practical literary criticism and creative writing not as crafts, but rather as philosophical enterprises. After all, the term *rowshanfekr* [intellectual] is almost a badge of honor in secular-minded circles in Iran. Some Persianists would appear to think that novelists, poets, and critics write great novels, compose classic lyric poems, and appreciate literary art to its fullest because of intellectual prowess. Perhaps because they think of literary activity as primarily intellectual and of literary critical activity as only secondarily a matter of research and discipline-specific methodology, they themselves are ready to speak and write about anything, from Ferdowsi to Dowlatabadi, from Nezami to Nima, from E'tesami to Farrokhzad. What surprises me is that what they write offers, more often than not, a good deal of food for thought and inspiration for more research-oriented and strictly literary critical study.

Afterwards, as Dr. Pourjavady's dinner guests, eight of us went to the Tandoor Restaurant, across the street from Amjadiyeh Stadium. We were the first customers for dinner. A waiter jumped up from the bench on one side of our table where he had been napping. A cockroach scurried across our table for cover. One of our group, apprehensive about Indian cuisine, kept asking if it came with plenty of rice. We ordered Tandoori chicken and chicken kabob, and lots of *mā'oshsha'ir*. The conversation was lively and at moments erudite. I briefly almost forgot I was foreign.

Tehran, Thursday, December 28th. Censorship of imaginative literature seems less stringent and comprehensive here today than during the Pahlavi era before 1977. Lively debates fill the pages of the most popular weeklies, monthlies, and quarterlies. A steady stream of novels and collections of poetry and short stories comes off the presses, the chief delay being scarcity of paper or the politics of its distribution. Despite high book prices relative to income and the devalued *riyāl*, printings of works on subjects from Hâfez to modern fiction sell out quickly. A new generation of critics and fiction writers has replaced the people I knew from the early 1970s, or at least joined those older writers.

The situation in poetry is less clearcut. Readers still hold Mehdi Akhavan-e Sales in great respect, as well as the memory of Nima Yushij. Shamlu's admirers think he has crossed the line between *she'r* [poetry] and *she'ār* [polemic(al) verse)] since the mid-1970s. They are noncommittal about such expatriate poets as Naderpour, Esma'il Kho'i, and Yadollah Ro'ya'i. A new generation of modernist poets has not attracted the spotlight the way Akhavan, Farrokhzad, Shamlu, and others did from the mid-1950s.

Every work of imaginative literature I know of is available in bookstores or from second-hand book dealers and sidewalk vendors. The works of Sadeq Hedayat and Forugh Farrokhzad may not get reprinted quickly any more, but are for sale in older editions and printings, as are the works of even such Tudeh writers in jail as M.E. Beh'azin.

Academics haven't the self-confidence of writers. Apprehensive about how classroom lectures and discussion might conflict with government ideology, they can receive written warnings if adminstrators get reports that classes have voiced heterodox ideas.

As for political discussion, at home, in offices, and elsewhere, people dissatisfied with government handling of products, services, and anything else express critical views openly, even anticlericism. They gripe about the lack of variety and quality of television shows, the price of foodstuffs, the long lines for food and buses, Islamic garb for women, the value of Iranian currency, traffic jams, air pollution, alleged corruption in various ministries, and foreign policy. University trained taxi drivers complain about the ruination in the 1980s of their professional aspirations and careers.

Except among family members and close acquaintances, expression of frank views on issues relating to the politics of government competence and performance did not take place in Pahlavi Iran from late 1953 to mid-1977. Such griping and criticism today do not bother clerical politicians because they do not expect divine guidance or inspiration in their management of the economy or traffic. In contrast, the Shah thought he knew more about most things than other people. His government considered it treasonous when anyone criticized policies which originated with him. The Shah's face appeared on more postage stamps than did any other image during his reign. In contrast, the first stamps with Khomeini's face on them have just appeared, after his death. In other words, he and his advisers understood why they should put images on stamps, not of him, but of everyday Iranians working and praying and fighting for the Revolution.

At the same time, penalties for activities meeting with official disapproval are routinely more serious now than in the Pahlavi era, and can occur without the equivalent of due process of law. Consumption of alcoholic beverages, anti-government political activity, flagrant violation of dress codes, and actions interpreted as insulting to Islam can lead to arrest, detention, interrogation, incarceration, and flogging. Dealing in narcotics can lead to the death penalty. Daily radio reports matter-of-factly list persons executed for drug trafficking.

Many educated Iranians maintain the same views and world views as they held before the Revolution. They have learned much in the 1980s and generally think life is more difficult today. They mostly blame the Pahlavi monarchy for their present difficulties. They think that the Shah deserved to fall and evidence embarrassment that they then tolerated and even kow-towed to such a small, mean-spirited man. In their view, American inter-ference in Iranian affairs, beginning with the unforgiv-able participation of the Eisenhower government in the overthrow of Mohammad Mosaddeq in August 1953 and ending with inexplicable support in the Reagan years for Iraq during the eight-year war, plays a major role in Iran's problems and will somehow haunt and dog America in the future. Iran Air would have one of the world's best safety records had not the American military blown one of its passenger jets out of the sky over the Persian Gulf last year.

Because people recognize that the Iran-Iraq war made government progress in reaching projected economic and social goals impossible, they are willing to wait before reaching a final judgement. Although few secular-minded Iranians expect religious leaders to be able to handle the economy and foreign affairs, most of them are willing to put up with such leadership for a long time. They got burned the last time they supported a revolution and will not get involved in politics that way again soon.

In any case, whoever is to rule in Iran, whether on his head rests a crown, a turban, or a military officer's hat, will face a daunting new millennium. If Tehran's problems long ago had to do with what its people needed but didn't have, many of its chief problems today have to do with what it has imported–automobiles, factories, technologies to house too many people in too small a space, equipment needing electricity, a subway which may never transport many Iranians. Modernization has Chernobylized Tehran, which desperately needs experts on pollution, transportation, water, electricity, and the other technical fields which modern life has called into play to deal with problems which industrialization and the capacity to import goods from abroad has created.

Intellectuals and bureaucrats talk of moving the capital to another location. But Tehran, with its population doubling every twenty years and its air unbreathable on many days, its noisy and noisome gridlock ubiquitous at certain times each day, and its poverty pervasive almost anywhere south of Shah Street, will remain on the brink of self-destruction. In all of this, the States needs to be ready to help. Regardless of political rhetoric and present official diplomatic non-communication, Washington, D.C. must know that the Iranian people are no better and no worse than people anywhere, that what happens to them and their environment affects life on the western side of the Atlantic. What is happening in and to Tehran is of equal significance to the situation in South American rain forests, to what happened to Chernobyl itself.

"Are you Iranian? No? From where then? America? Have you room in your suitcase?" "Friend, if one has family and good friends, places are not important. Besides"– and I momentarily almost mean what I say and can afford to say it because of that little royal blue passport in my shirt pocket–"your food and poetry and history and *khâk-e pâk-e irân* [Iran's pure earth] exist nowhere else."

The fact is that I am ready right now to call the telephone taxi to take me to the airport to bring to an end these dilettantish days so markedly in contrast with the dead serious, mortally serious, sometimes fatally serious business of Iranian living here. Every family has a story of death, in the Revolution, in the war, or of a future suddenly changed, of families here, in Pakistan, in Turkey, everywhere.

Hamed Raziee and Ghassem Khosravan rang Maliheh's front door bell at eight this morning. Afzal had called them to say that I was in town and to have them tell me that he would not be able to come to Tehran himself. Sixteen years of not seeing one another over in a minute, we talked for an hour, and met again at Hamed's for dinner tonight. Hamed's "little son" Mohammad, who came to Eliza's birthday party in 1972, is finishing his university engineering degree this coming spring. The three Razi'ee girls are polite and vivacious. Hamed's wife, whom I don't think I saw in Mashhad and whom I met just once or twice in Reza'iyeh, asked after Sorayya and pored over family snapshots with interest. Hamed, whose specialty is applied linguistics, teaches French at several Tehran universities. After all these years, he quickly located snapshots from the days when he was my student at Mashhad University, including a photograph I had signed for him in 1966.

As for Ghassem, he is doing okay, but has struggled to stay afloat during the past ten years. At the outset of the Revolution, his prior employment with the American government haunted him in the form of unfounded allegations of past association with the Iranian secret police. His oldest son is now studying in Holland. In some ways discouraged, Ghassem nevertheless seems determined to make it and to make sense out of what the Revolution has done to his career.

Mehrâbâd Airport, Tehran, Saturday, December 30th.
Here in the waiting lounge, two hundred or so Iranians and one American are waiting to board Lufthansa Flight 601. A glass of wine, a nap and a breakfast from now, Sarvar will be driving me from Frankfurt to Göttingen. Four days there, a week in Paris, back to Göttingen, and on to Austin by January 15th. By then, my days here will have begun to merge with earlier years in Iran, alive on their own, but like memories of my father which flesh him out as simultaneously middle-aged and old. Iran is now two Irans for me.

Goodbyes at the apartment were not emotional. Maliheh and the children were thinking about Abbas who called in midafternoon from Istanbul after nearly a month of no news. The call relieved Maliheh who said he sounded okay and was planning a quick return to Tehran even if unable to arrange an American visa for his friend in Turkey. The two of them have also visited Dubai, Cyprus, and Athens in their effort to get that visa. The family is worried sick that Abbas is less worried about his heart condition than about his friend's visa.

Earlier this evening–I got here hours ahead of time to take in the airport scene–the customs inspector downstairs told me that the ten small packets of saffron which friends and relatives gave me for Sorayya could not leave the country. I asked him to imagine Sorayya's disappointment when she learns that none of her relatives and friends in Tehran have sent her anything. I reminded him of the special meaning of gifts travellers take to Iranian friends and relatives far away, especially in these days of misunderstandings between his country and mine. After a pause, the official gestured with his hand and a dismissive look of impatience. I put the saffron back into the suitcase, drew a deep breath, and began my defense of the books, fifteen or twenty on literary subjects, which he had also declared forbidden to leave the country.

"I need these books for my work," I say, "work which may help Americans appreciate Iran. In addition, many of the books are gifts." I pick out one, an edition of Ferdowsi's story of Siyâvash which Mahmud Borujerdi gave me after my lecture at the Tehran Philosophical Society. I suggest that the customs officer call Society Director Borujerdi (whose name apparently registered with him) to tell him that his gift to me cannot leave the country. Again a pause, after which the customs officer rolled his eyes, turned to the passenger behind me, and said, "Next." I closed my suitcase, saffron and books inside, and felt content and grateful. I realized that no such exchanges take place at Kennedy or Los Angeles International airports.

But contentment didn't last long, because one thing did not make it through customs: my research and interview notes, mostly in a seventy-page reporter's notebook, and photographs of literary figures and events. Yet their confiscation, which means I can't finish *An Iranian Mullah's Son*, has not perturbed me. The loss is only an added admission charge to a Tehran I needed to walk around in.

No announcement yet, but all Lufthansa passengers except for the American are gathering their things and assembling near the door to the buses. Our Airbus is not in sight, but is out there in the darkness. I've made mental notes on women's attire and head coverings to appreciate their much discussed transformation in appearance which occurs once Lufthansa flights from Tehran are airborne. No doubt many passengers, I among them, will then quickly, but with feigned nonchalance, order a cocktail, beer, or wine. Of course, we'll have to order food and drink in English or German. Lufthansa flight attendants don't speak Persian. Moreover, in-flight radio and television programs air in German, English, Arabic, and Pashto, the last two languages an apparent concession to passengers who perhaps seem indistinguishable from Arabs and

Afghans to Western airline officialdom. Such otherwise inconsequential details intimate how difficult it is to be Iranian, especially for Iranians with my views living in the Tehran to which I'll bid adieu momentarily. I am looking forward to breakfast on the plane.

Epilogue

My brother-in-law Abbas flew home from Istanbul in early January 1990, while I was with my sister-in-law Fahimeh and her husband Sarvar in Göttingen. At the university there, I gave a talk to Iranian students on impressions from my weeks in Tehran. Just weeks later back in Austin, word reached us that Abbas was dead of a heart attack. When I talked with Yashar on the telephone a day or two after, he asked only about my next trip to Tehran.

In late February 1990, a manila envelope marked with the name of an engineering firm in the Chamber of Commerce Building in Pittsburgh reached my Persepolis Enterprises mailbox in Austin. The envelope contained the research notes and photographs confiscated at the Tehran's Mehrabad Airport on December 30th.

In April 1990 I flew to San Francisco for a weekend, mainly to hear a talk at UC Berkeley by Ahmad Shamlu. He stunned an audience of upwards of eight hundred people (who had paid eight dollars apiece to hear him talk) by mocking that part of Iranian cultural history which revolves around kingship, reminding the audience of the cruelty of Sasanid king Anusharvan whom Iranians routinely (and with unintended irony) call "The Just."

Shamlu also turned Ferdowsi's *Shâhnâmeh* upside down and, expanding a thesis he had presented a decade earlier in *Ketâb-e jom'eh*, suggested Zahhak as a man from the people whom establishment patriarchal and royalist writers and other authorities from long before Ferdowsi had distorted into a despicable and despotic usurper. Iranians everywhere have rejected Shamlu's thesis in scores of articles and letters condemning his attack on their mythological and historical family tree.

Shamlu's literary career rankles some Iranian academics who find his popularity and self-assured iconoclasm infuriating, especially because he has no university training and because he dismisses formal Persian studies as so much grave-robbing. Esfahan University Persian professor Mehdi Nourian, whose tenure as a visiting scholar at Texas during the 1990-1991 academic year Nasrollah Pourjavady had me arrange, categorically la-

bels Shamlu "*bisavâd*" [illiterate] and asserts that the poet
literally has no right to talk or write on Hafez or
Ferdowsi. Nourian is dead certain–even broken clocks
"confidently" tell correct time twice a day–that Khanlari's
traditionalist verse composition called "Oqâb" [The Eagle]
is much superior to any Shamlu "poem." Academics like
Nourian are exasperated by the facts that many university
students hold the opposite view and that Shamlu can draw
overflow audiences wherever he talks, while a professor
talking on the same subject can't fill a seminar room.

In July and August 1990, while teaching two Persian
literature courses at Portland State University, I lectured
twice on my trip to Tehran. Once was at the Returned Peace
Corps Volunteer Conference at Eugene. The atmosphere
there reminded me that many Peace Corps people have
distinctive outlooks because of special cross-cultural experiences, of knowing America from the outside, of seeing
technology and nationalism for what they are. My second
talk was at PSU. Seated by herself in the left corner of the
lecture hall was an American mother of two young children whose Iranian architect husband had died of brain
cancer just days earlier.

At the November 1990 meeting of the Middle East
Studies Association in San Antonio, I mounted an exhibition of twenty-four recent paintings by Nasser Ovissi. In
them, Achaemenid and Sasanid icons, Arabic calligraphy
and Koranic phrases, Sufistic content, royal miniature-
painting subjects and styles, Qajar images, European subjects and shapes, and motifs from *saqqâkhânehs* [water-
drinking alcoves in traditional neighborhoods] have no
difficulty occupying the same visual arena. But Ovissi
perhaps does not achieve an integration or synthesis of
themes in his paintings. His characteristically Iranian
ambivalent eclecticism makes possible their sparkling
optimism and contributes to their colorful prettiness.

We used the gallery site one evening for poetry readings
in memory of Mehdi Akhavan-e Sales who had died in
Tehran a month earlier. Simin Behbahani and Nader
Naderpour recited new poems of their own at the gathering. Back in Tehran, in response to an interviewer's question about Persian studies in the States, Behbahani was
quoted in *Donyâ-ye sokhan* as saying: "Michael
Hillmann, with the encouragement of his Iranian spouse,
has published a selection of poems by Forugh

Farrokhzad." Back in Los Angeles, Naderpour wrote me that future editions of *Iranian Culture: A Persianist View* should acknowledge him as the source of some of its ideas.

Our quiet Austin spring this year got a needed lift with a one-day visit by Ahmad Shamlu. At a public talk and poetry reading at the University before an audience of three hundred-fifty people and later at a dinner at Mansur Taghehchian's, he continued his iconoclastic assault on traditionalist and establishment values. Middle-aged and older Iranian males at both gatherings were mostly aghast. To a question of mine about Parsipur's *Women without Men*, Mr. Shamlu replied: "The book is nothing, absolutely nothing. Anyone who writes like that with images of vaginas is crazy."

Harvard University's Center for Middle Eastern Studies has published an article of mine called "An Autobiographical Voice–Forugh Farrokhzad" in a volume called *Women's Autobiographies in Contemporary Iran* (1991). A reference in one of my footnotes to "bardolatrous" features of the biographical sketch in Mostafa Farzaneh's *Âshnâ'i bâ sâdeq hedâyat* [Acquaintance with Sadeq Hedayat] (1985) appears as "barbarous" because of an editor's emandation. I hope Mr. Farzaneh, who is less capable of barbarousness than almost anyone I know, accepts my explanation of how the wrong word got into the footnote. My surname appears on the book's front cover with one 'n'.

A month ago, on July 4th, as America brought to a climax celebrations of victory in the Desert Storm campaign against Iraq, I left Austin for Tehran and ten more days of walking and talking and reflecting. Conversations with Reza Baraheni, Mahmud Dowlatabadi, Nasrollah Pourjavady, Yann Richard, and Bo Utas were highlights of my brief stay, which I'll likely write about some time before long. I made inquiries this trip about teaching again in Tehran some time soon. No one asked me any questions at the airport this time, even when I lugged fifty kilograms of books in two suitcases through Customs to the Lufthansa counter. Lufthansa now makes in-flight announcements in Persian, as well as in English and German. Tehran seemed much changed since 1989, its economic and social problems worse and its up-town population more adjusted or resigned to things.

In late July, Voice of America broadcast a Persian "translation" in Iran of an article of mine which had appeared in *Iran Peace Corps Association Newsletter* #4. Called "Tehran, A Revolution Later," the article comprised snippets from Part 2 of this book. However, Voice of America, which had not consulted me about using the article, passed off my observations about Tehran in 1989 as if they had to do with mid-1991. Morever, the broadcast put a curious spin on my words, which hints at new American government aims in relations with Iran.

The broadcast misquotes me as observing a very kind look on the face of an Iranian passport official at the Tehran airport. It also misquotes me as reporting that a Hezbollâh official at the airport ended his interrogation of me with a "welcome to Iran." Voice of America goes on to misrepresent my written impressions by misquoting me as saying that I thought of the airport official who examined my luggage, accompanied me to my hotel, looked at my telephone messages, and watched me unpack in my room as "kind" and as "a new-found friend." The broadcast reports me as saying that once I reached my Tehran hotel I no longer felt as if foreign or out of place. The broadcast even asserts that I thought of official reactions to my arrival and presence in Tehran as evidence of "wonted Iranian hospitality," presumably including the armed paramilitary men who stopped my taxicab one evening and interrogated me. The broadcast also fabricates a description of grand American Peace Corps achievements in Iran as coming out of my mouth, while I have never thought that the Peace Corps in Iran served more than to educate PCVs and enrich our subsequent lives. The Voice of America broadcast did not report any of my anecdotes about unofficial Iranians and their heart-warming hospitality.

I've shelved my Âl-e Ahmad biography project and am busy with a new book on Hafez, planning for a lecture series next spring called "Iran, A Revolution Later," and coordination of a conference in April called "Iran and the New World Order."